Social Transformation
through Personal Transformations
The why and how of "being the change you wish to see in the world"

This book is structured in the like manner that one comes to understand and apply the things of it. Our hope is that by the end of it, one will both realize the *why* of this order, and will, with this order, order one's life accordingly.

> I. We start with talking about why true social transformation can only occur through collective personal transformations.
>
> II. We then go on to elaborate some of the core philosophies that make these transformations possible and suggest to what end these transformations be directed.
>
> III. Next, we describe how the actual process of transformation occurs in an individual's life and how this translates to the individual's collective community.
>
> IV. Lastly, we will discuss both the urgency and importance of the promulgation of these ideas into the world and into the lives of those who are building the foundations for the future.

Copyright © 2014 Greg Wurm

All rights reserved.

Cover photo courtesy Joy Prior, Becky Leung, and Jeanie Thatcher.

Printed by Y Mountain Press.

Contact the Author:
greg@changetheworldcoaching.com

Contents

Part I
Why true social transformation can only occur through collective personal transformations.

1. The *Why* of "Why?" – Why asking "why?" is not only insightful, but critical 9
2. The Possibility and Probability of *True* Change 12
3. Inter-independence – The Next New Old Concept 16
4. The Nature and Nurture of Society 19
5. *True* Progress – What It Is and Is Not 24
6. Society's Weakest Link(s) 28
7. Social Transformation—
   An Achievement or a Condition? 31
8. Personal Transformation into Social Beings............... 38
9. The *True* and *Only* Way to Change the World 42

Part II
We then go on to elaborate some of the core philosophies that make these transformations possible, as well as suggest to what end these transformations be directed.

10. The *Why* of This *Why*—Core Philosophies 49
11. The Different Way of Thinking—Eternity, Infinity, and Spirituality 52
12. Ontology of Humans... 56
13. Epistemology of Our Approach 62
14. Man's Ontology and God's Ontotheology................... 66

15. Idealism and Realism— Why having a small vision is sometimes best	70
16. Who is a Change Maker?	73
17. A-ethical Ethics	75
18. The Ideal Way to Find the Ideal	78
19. Duty of Love and Love of Duty	82
20. The Sameness of the Healthy	85
21. Principles of a Healthy Society	88
22. Social Self-Control	92
23. The Structural Level of the Social Self of the Individual	96
24. Against Againstness and For Forness	100
25. What Would You Do if There Were No World to Change?	103
26. Personal and Social Processes of Teaching and Learning	107
27. Trust In and Work Towards Transformation	111
28. Stop Trying to Change the World	115
29. Accepting the World as Changed	119

Part III

Next, we describe how the actual process of transformation occurs in an individual's life and how this translates to the individual's collective community.

30. The *Why* of "How?"	125
31. What Is Transformation and How Does it Work?	129
32. Transforming Agent and Agent of Transformation	132
33. Hierarchy of Consumption	136
34. A Change of Heart	140
35. Personal Transformation Through Social Transformations	144

36. Personal Transformations Through Social
    Transformation 148
37. Habits and Culture—Doing and Becoming 152
38. Becoming Together 155
39. Gift and Exchange 159

Part IV
Lastly, we will discuss both the urgency and importance of the promulgation of these ideas into the world and into the lives of those who are building the foundations for the future.

40. The *Why* of This *Why*—Urgency and Importance 165
41. What Is Important and What Is Urgent? 168
42. What You *Need* to Know 172
43. *Promulgation*—How to Share 175
44. With Whom to Share 178
45. The Builders, the Builder, the Built 181
46. The Role of the Material World In Social Change 185
47. When Will People Change? 189
48. Why Nothing Else is As Important or As Urgent 192
49. The One Choice 196

Preface

It is the nature of challenges that they can tell us our true nature. And, it is also their nature to change our natures. They both make us better and reveal that which is best about us. For it has been said, "Champions aren't made in the ring, but merely recognized there." Thus, the completion of a boxing match is also the completion of the boxer. It is likewise so with any book and it's author, and in particular has been this case with this book.

"I write because I don't know what I think until I read what I say." - Flannery O'Conner

Most books write themselves long before the author them self actually starts writing them. Like all action, both verbal and nonverbal, they spring forth from thought. Thoughts which come from life experience, deep contemplation, and divine inspiration. These thoughts are given form and crystallized in books, but likewise do not become crystallized in the Author's own mind until they receive this, their latter form.

It has been said that a man's philosophy is his own autobiography. Thus, an idea cannot come from an author that has not come to the author in some way previous or present to when the author authorizes the legitimacy of the idea into the palatable and replicable pages of a book. 'Therefore, yes these ideas come from the author, but have not necessarily come for me, the author. As the above quote at the beginning of the preface stated, I sometimes had no idea what I was saying until it was being said. Therefore, in one sense I do not claim to be the author, but more the mediator of the ideas. And, a book is merely a medium through which a mediator can mediate.

Throughout the book, though I the author am one, the pronoun *we* was used. To justify as to why *I* used *we* would be helpful to both you and us in that you will see that the *we* is reflexive and dyadic. From a strictly grammatical point, the *we* can be appropriate and that it is being used as the "Royal We." But, from a more philosophical perspective, the *we* is used in that it is intended to be collective in its output as it is in its input.

The book was not written by me to you, but by we for us, which includes me. This is the essence of not knowing what you think until you read what you say. It is revealed to you as you reveal it to others. If I am truly a benefactor of its writing, then you the reader are and were truly a contributor to its creation as well. For it is you, the world, which includes me, that this book is intended to change and whom I had in mind when writing the book.

This book was written to change the world. And yes, that large scope has been part of what has made this so challenging. But, in reality, anything less than this might have been more of a challenge in the end. John F. Kennedy once said, "The only reason to give a speech is to change the world." Is the same here with this. The only reason, for me, to write a book is to change the world. It is in this book that we give an introduction, body, and conclusion to an idea that true social transformation can only occur through collective personal transformations. All of the parts of this thesis will be discussed throughout, but in order for the reader to get through it, they first have to get to it.

Many people might stop reading here with such a one-sided notion that this is the true and only way to change the world, but we invite our readers to consider this notion. We discuss in the book further what we mean by true and also its accompanying adverb, *only*. *Only* often entails singularity, but here it pertains more to actuality. Meaning, the *only* way the world actually changes is through personal changes. Any other changes that are made in the world are incomplete, unrealized and therefore not fully actualized or truly actual.

It is in the realization of each person that we as a people will be realized. That is our main argument, our central premise, or our thesis and proposition.

It only makes sense, therefore, that this realization of this proposition came in a moment of realization to me, the propositor, in that a book to change the world has come from a change in my world.

In January 2010, my life changed in an instant. I do not have a jaw-dropping story to relate, except that ironically the story does relate to my jaw dropping. I was living downtown in Detroit, Michigan, in and among many of its lower-income minority members. I went on this day in January to an auto show that was downtown in one of the city's central convention centers.

Upon entering the building and seeing a display of such contrasted wealth and whiteness, my jaw dropped and literally made a popping noise. I thought nothing of it at the time, but not a day has gone by since then that my life has not been influenced by it.

To make a long story short, this jaw-dropping experience somehow translated itself into my physical being in the form of a physical ailment. I called it a problem with my eye. Whenever I used my eye to read or focus, I would get a pressure behind it that would escalate until the point of complete incapability. Literally, it is a headache that prompts dizziness and nausea if I do not follow its prompting to stop doing the things that start it, namely reading.

Not being able to read or function in the same way I could previously led me to start the journey to find out what was wrong with my eye. It is through the journey that I learned that the problem was not with my eye, but with me. My "eye" was not the problem, "I" was. I had identified the wrong "I/eye" as the problem.

There was another day when I was frustrated with the lack of solutions to my problem and the unsustainability of positive thinking to make me better that I, in my head, screamed out to God, "I don't care about feeling better, I just want to be better." Feeling better internally was not as important to me at that time as being better externally or physically. Yet, quickly came God's quaint rebuke, when He said, "You won't *feel* better physically, until you *be* better spiritually." Or, to change the external you have to change the internal.

That is the paradigm of the premise throughout the pages of this book. The world cannot be any better than the world is itself. That is, the visible external world that we can see and interact with through our bodies and its senses, cannot transform itself anymore than transformations that occur in the internal worlds of the people who we see and interact with through our bodies and our senses. It is the invisible changes that become visible, and the lack of them that is likewise visible.

That is the observation I've seen and made, and I believe I am not alone in this induction. How much of the world today is tattered by terrifying scenes of civil unrest or the perishing impoverished. The social ills are real, but the pills we give society are merely helping the society to "feel better, but not be better." It is as positive thinking was to me, unsustainable.

The call of transformation is to be better; to not just mask the symptoms of dysfunction, but to become complete or whole. To change to an unchangeable form, which is a new form entirely, and therefore merits the word "*tran*s-form." I have found that as I act in a transformed way, my eye problem becomes irrelevant. So will the problems with society dissipate themselves out of existence when we, as a society, transform ourselves.

This book is for anyone who wants to transform the world in any way. The ways are as endless as are the configurations of men and women in the world. You can use this book for you and you alone.

For those who do this, this book is merely a self-help book. This is not bad on its own, because by helping yourself you help all, but you will find that your own personal transformation is tied up inseparably with the transformation of others, both as individuals and as a collective. Therefore, this book is more than a self-help, but an all-help. It embraces the paradox of the three musketeers, "All for One and One for All."

Maybe you have a business or an organization that is struggling? The concepts in this book pertain to you, for a business can be no better than are its businessmen. Maybe you are the principal of a school? A school can be no better than are the students and the teachers in the school.

You can have the fanciest new equipment, or the ageless architecture of centuries before, but if the students themselves do not become the fancy, new, and ageless architects of their own lives and education, the school will quickly become as outdated, ugly and aged as the morale of the students and teachers.

This book applies to cities, states, and nations in any civic organization or community, that by its very nature is a social entity in its entirety. But, most of all, this book applies to the social organization that is most of all, that is the world.

Maybe, it's hard to see the world as a social organization because of its visibly unorganized appearance, but it is in the disorder that we see an order that is unseen. This unseen order is an order and its name is "*dis*". We can label it as dis-order, but knowing it is in disorder implies that we have some sense of what order *should* look like. This is an order that is moral in nature and is disputed, but only superficially. This order is what we are trying to establish. We cannot order the world to order, but can only invite it to order itself. This book has been written in order to do this, in order to order. To say what is the right order, why it is the right order, and how we order ourselves rightly to it.

As I said at the beginning of the Preface, writing this book has been a challenge. It is one of the visible aspects of my own personal process that is finally being put in a tangible form. Its content is the content which has filled the inner pages of my soul for some time and now is out for the public to take what they wish. The ideas are only as powerful as you let them be for you as they were not as powerful to me until I let them out of me. That is the challenge of being a good writer and a good reader. And, that is the challenge of becoming a better challenger to the mighty task ahead of both yours, mine, or our personal and social transformations.

I

Why true social transformation can only occur through collective personal transformations

Why must each transformation
only occur through a linear
perceptual transformation.

Chapter 1

The *Why* of "Why?"

Why asking "why?" is not only insightful, but critical

Why have we decided to start the first section of the first chapter of the first part of this book with the discussion on the concept of *why*?

Why is an interesting question in that it prompts one to look deeper into one's motives and reasons for why they do the things they do. Once this motive or reason has been determined, one can ask why this is even one's motive in the first place. Once an answer to this question is given, one can ask why this answer was given and thus any question emerges.

Why then do we start with the question of *why* here when we have not even made a statement to ask *why* for? In the next chapter, we will go into more detail about the *why* of the argument in this book, regarding social and personal transformations, but here we have found it useful to start with a mini discourse on why understanding this *why* is so essential. This is to prep you for the prepping that the next section will prep you for. The next section is to prep you for the rest of the book and this section is to prep you for the next section.

It is our hope that you will find that every next section is to prep you for the next section. At the end of the book, the preparation will be for a section that is not found within the book, but must be written within your own world. This next section is meant to be created by the reader through their actions and what history they record with them.

Why do we as humans care about the *why* of our actions? What is it about the reasons behind a given task that changes the way we give ourselves to the task?

The task of this book is to help show and explain why social transformation can only occur through personal transformations, and like we explained before, the task of the next section is to explain why this last statement is true, and the task of this section is to explain why we even need to explain why the statement is true in the first place.

Maybe we could even have a section before this that attempts to explain why we are asking the *why* about our *why*? And maybe even before that, a section could be written about the *why* of the *why* of the *why* and so on. We could ask why to infinity, but why should we?

Asking *why* allows you to enter deeper into the assumptions you make in life. Some of these assumptions, if not all of them, have been learned and are so embedded within our subconscious that we hardly consider them when making choices. When we take the time to first reflect on why we do the things we do in the way we do them, it allows us to see the path of assumptions that have been learned and have led us to the beliefs and attitudes we currently hold.

Now is this always essential to do before every action? No. A lot of our assumptions and the things we have learned have served us well, and will continue to serve us well.

The reason why you would dive into the *why* of your actions is that your actions are no longer serving you. You question your approach only when it doesn't get you the results you wish for. You might even be considered "insane" if you don't.

The question, "What results do we even want?" is vital in knowing what actions you need to take. This is sometimes called the Goal Expectancy Theory. Are the actions you are taking instrumental in achieving the outcome you value? Can you expect to achieve your current goal on the path you are currently on? You could ask *why* you want the results you want, and you could ask *why* you believe a certain path to be the best path that leads to those results.

Are the outcomes or results we want most in life taught to us throughout the various socialization processes we undergo from childhood to now? Or, are these outcomes or results universal and inherent in the very beings we are as humans? This is essentially the nature versus nurture debate. However, this debate is more of a dialogue of friends today than a heated dispute of enemies of the past. Most people believe that it's not nature versus nurture, but nature *and* nurture.

We both *learn* what to want, and have tendencies wired in us at birth to *know* what to want. But, the question is, "is why we want the things we want a matter of nature or nurture?" We can assume that most people want to be happy. But, can we assume that most people want to be happy for the same reasons? Maybe reasons and motives are just as universal and inherent as they are learned through various nurturing processes. But, why does this even matter?

Why it matters is for two reasons: one, we have a universal and inherent nature; and two, this nature can be nurtured into whatever we wish.

Maybe our nature is just as dynamic as is our potential to learn and grow? Maybe learning and growing is merely the evolving of our natures? Maybe we inherit a nature at a certain place and can evolve or devolve it given both our environment and choice in how we respond to it? Thus, when we ask *why* we look into our nature and into our nurturing. Whatever can be learned can be unlearned and whatever our predisposition is can be disposed of in service to the higher being we are capable of becoming.

Therefore, when we ask why and why and *why*, we are asking people to look deeper into the world they've been given in order to understand more fully the world they live in. It is only once people understand *their* world that they can understand *the* world. And, understanding both worlds is critical for anyone who wants to change them. This is the reason we ask *why*.

Chapter 2

The Possibility and Probability of *True* Change

In the previous chapter, we discussed why we ask why in the first place. Now that we have gained further insight into this "inq-why-ry," we will commence with the answering of the why of the main proposition of this book, namely as the title suggests, that of social transformation through personal transformations.

Why can true social transformation occur only through collective personal transformations? It helps first to describe why we use the word "true."

There is always true change and then there is the illusion of change. But, to understand what true change is, we have to understand what it is that is being changed in order to merit the word *true* as its adverb.

True change is always sustainable. But, just that it is sustainable doesn't mean that it *can't* crash and burn, but that it *won't*. In the world of possibility in which we live, there is always the possibility for something to occur.

If we negated chance its opportunity to exist, we would at the same time obliterate the chance for opportunity to exist as well. If it wasn't possible for change not to occur, then it would be possible for change to occur. Therefore, sustainability doesn't mean that something can never become unsustainable again, it just means that it won't.

We have also been careful not to use the word *probably* in this description. We were tempted to say, "It doesn't mean that something can never be unsustainable again, it just means that it PROBABLY won't."

True change does not occur in the world of probability, because true change is 100%. One-hundred-percent probability is possibility. If something is 100% improbable that we would classify as impossible. If something is 100% positively probable, that we would classify it as 100% possible.

Possibility is a lot stronger of a force than we ever think. We often think that possibility is only a last resort type of word, when you want something but all the odds are against you, but you maintain some hope or possibility. However, possibility is and should be our first source of confidence in our pursuit for what we want.

In the realm of wanting change, we must always keep in mind that change for the better is always possible and change for the worse is always likewise. But, true 100% change is so true and complete that even though it is still possible for the change to be undone, it is at the same time impossible due to the trueness and completeness of the change.

That might seem to be a paradox, and you're probably right. The greatest truths are always found within great paradoxes. Thinking within these paradoxes is not always easy, but with a new understanding of the word "true," we would argue that it is the only "true" thinking there actually is. All other type of thinking is merely an illusion.

Therefore, true change is change that is both permanent but not impermeable. The full amount and measure of choice that goes into bringing about such full and almost immeasurable quantities of change can be exercised in its reverse to undo and make incomplete again which was previously made complete and completed.

True social transformation will be complete once there has been a complete completion of personal transformations. Thus, the only way to change the world is to change the worlds of those in the world.

People can exist independent of a society, but a society emerges only out of the existence of more than one person who comes to the knowledge of the other and interaction occurs between them. There could be no such thing as a society if there were no people in it and or of it.

People are what make the world. The world is not what makes people. However, within this last statement is a truth about the world's potential to make people that must be considered and will be discussed.

Though the world does not make people, it can. Now that might not make sense, but much like our conversation above, about true change and illusory change, it takes a level of "true" thinking to understand this.

We could argue the opposite of the point we just made. In a sense, the world can and does make people. But, only when these people allow it. Thus, in allowing the world to make them it can look like the world is making them, but they themselves are the ones who are making themselves. The world can stimulate them to make themselves in a certain way, but does not determine them to be made in a certain way.

People always have the choice of how they want to be made and what they want to make of themselves. Therefore, the world and the state of it with all of its conditions, circumstances, and social forces can and sometimes does influence the process of how people are made, but does not cause indeterminably the making of people.

Those who do let the world make them completely and entirely will bear the image of the world. Those who choose to not let themselves be at the mercy of the world's shaping influence will often bear the image of something or someone greater. Often themselves, but sometimes divinity.

Though there is not a causal relationship in the direction from world to man, does this causality and determinant force exist in the reverse? Does the social world exist as a direct relationship with the relationships of the people in the said world?

Can we know with certainty that collective personal transformations would actually yield a true social transformation? What assumptions are we making in regards to society and its true nature and function?

Just like people have a nature and a nurture, what role does nurturing play in the development of a society? Does society exist *sui generis* and independent of people as a thing in itself? Is it a thing at all or is it living? Meaning, should we look at society as an object or as an organism? All these questions will be addressed in the next chapter.

Chapter 3

Inter-independence— The Next New Old Concept

There is a popular behaviorist philosophy that thinks if you could have absolute control over a man's environment, you could have absolute control over the man. This is the idea that we dissected above. This idea is the same idea that says the world makes the man. Not that the world can have influence in the shaping of the man, but that it absolutely causally creates, makes, and shapes the man with no option of the man through this process but to be acted upon.

The converse of this ideology would empower the man with choice to determine both his own destiny and his own world. This idea would say that if you could have absolute control over a man, you would have absolute control over his environment.

Now, the idea of absolute control over a man is also an idea that needs some evaluation. It would also be a behaviorist belief to believe that you could have absolute control over a man and they would do this through attempting to control his environment. However, even the non-behaviorist believes in absolute control over a man, but it would not come through his environment but through his consent.

A man can give himself to another to control him and this is why we often seem to think that the environment or circumstances in which we are in have such control over us. They only control us as far as we let them. But, also true is that we can control them as much as we wish to.

Going beyond the idea of having absolute control over a man is the idea of a man having absolute control over himself. This would be an even more evolved state of control. The first idea would give a man completely to the control of another, while the second idea would give a man completely to the control of himself.

Now, the paradox is, what if both were possible at the same time? This is the idea behind Stephen Covey's concept of interdependence and one of the foundational ideas and understanding the true nature of society.

When you are a child or a baby in your most undeveloped state your parents have almost complete control over you. As you develop you grow in your capacity to control yourself. This is growing from dependence to independence.

All people go from stage to stage at different rates in different parts of their lives. There are some children who are more independent in one aspect of their life as an adult is in their life and some adults that are more dependent in parts of their life than a child is in theirs.

A society of all dependent people would and could never work. All people would die or never be able to live in the first place. A society of all independent people would and could never even be considered a society. People would not die, because they can take care of themselves, but they would all live independent and separate lives thus failing to meet the most crucial of criteria for creating a society.

A society is formed and begins at the state of interdependence between two people. This is often called the joint good. This theory states that both parties are dependent upon by the other party for some good that they could not attain alone and thus they are dependent upon each other for the receiving of this joint good.

However, we wonder if there is yet another level or stage in this development. Maybe, the next stage would be inter-independence?

What would this look like and how would it be operative in the world?

Two parties in interdependence with each other is synonymous with a society being as a person in the dependent stage. Two parties in inter-independence would be synonymous with a society being as a person in the independent stage. This is the state of true social transformation and can only come from a collective state of independence of all people who make up the state.

Remember, it is not just independence of the people themselves, because like we said before that does not make a society, but it is independence of the relationships between the people themselves. People enter into relationships not because they are dependent upon the other for the attainment of some joint good, but because they simply want to.

With the word and idea of dependence we use the words, "have to, obligation, or necessity." Yet, with inter-independent relationships people don't need each other, they want each other. They do not enter into agreements out of obligation, but out of love. They do not have to work together to get something they want to have, but to give something they want to give.

The interaction from which a society emerges is voluntary and thus under the complete control of the actors themselves. Therefore, true social transformation can never be forced, but only possible through the choices of people who have been personally transformed to the development stage of inter-independence. It is yet another reason why true social transformation can only occur through collective personal transformations.

Chapter 4

The Nature and Nurture of Society

We raised a couple of questions at the end of chapter two. Is society something that exists independent and *sui generis* of the individual actors in it? Or, does it function in itself in a way comparable to the way an individual functions as an individual in themselves? Can there be similarities drawn between the nature and nurture debate in science to the social world from a perspective that looks at the social world as an entity in itself? All of these questions we will attempt to answer here.

When we ask, "what is society?" We can answer the question both as if society was a noun and if it was a verb. Looking at it as a noun would be a very Greek way of understanding the concept of society. But, when we look at words and concepts as verbs, we are understanding it more Hebraically.

For the Greeks, to understand an object was to get down to its very essence, or its perfect metaphysical form. Nothing in reality could actually represent this and therefore to truly understand anything, one would need to escape the material world and enter into the metaphysical world of forms.

For the Hebrews, they look at an object in terms of its usefulness, or its activity. It is what it is used for, and from what is gained by its use that determines its character. For example, someone who was thinking like a Greek would consider a couch to be just that—a couch—no matter where it is or what it's used for. Thinking

Hebraically, a couch can become a bed if it is used to sleep on more so if used for that purpose regularly.

The verb form of "society" would thus change the word slightly to that of "societing", and the noun it might be helpful to consider as "societiness." What is the essence of society, and what is it doing?

As we stated above, society doesn't exist independent of people. People can exist without it, but it cannot exist without people. However though this is true, once people do get together and form either interdependence or inter-independent relationships a new and separate reality emerges.

This social phenomenon can act as a person upon a person, the like we discussed in the previous chapter, the person still chooses how they let it act upon them. The person chooses this by the way they see it. Therefore, society merely exists in the perceptions of each individual person. The society I know and see is different than the society you observe.

Thus, society does exist independent of people, but not their perceptions. However, whatever the collective perception is could be a good indicator of what we could use as an instrument to help us understand the nature or true essence of society.

Thinking of society as an instrument only turns it into an object. Though this is true, there is also more to consider. Just like we have bodies, which are essentially assorted elements of the earth, which is likewise the common component in objects, we are not just objects. We have something living within us that moves us and is not able to be associated with the defining attribute of objectness. We are subjects too. We can perceive ourselves as objects and others as objects just like we can perceive society to be only an object.

But, is it a mistake to exclude from our conversation the idea of society or the world being likewise comparable to the subject nature of man?

We often hear of the word and concept of collective consciousness to describe in some way the essence of what we're talking about. It seems like there are universal perceptions of society that we all share that collectively make whatever these perceptions are seem and become true.

Therefore, the nature of society can operate under similar laws under which we as individual actors operate, because society is merely a collection and a completion of these shared realities and perceptions.

Looking at society from the perspective of one person born into the world we realize that when they are born they supposedly inherit a nature that becomes inherent within them. At the same time they are born, society is born for them as they begin to interact and engage with it and the actors in it external to them. Therefore, they only understand the nature of society through the process of what they learn about it from it and from others. The nature of society for them is not fixed but evolves as they grow up and grow into their own specific role and function they play in it.

It would be false to assume that society doesn't exist in itself before they were born, but only exists for them once they are born. Therefore, every time someone is born and learns to interact in a way to create a social reality, the reality of the social world becomes more real.

The nature of society is both fixed and dynamic. It is fixed in how it comes about, but is dynamic in what comes about. This dynamicness is because that which brings it about is not fixed in their natures. The humans to create society are not deterministic causal beings according to behaviorist philosophies as was discussed previously.

What comes about through the actors is what changes society. Change always comes from within and the within part of a society is its people. The within part of an individual actor is the individual actor in which all individuals are patterned after.

From the Christian tradition, being created in God, we find the kingdom of God within us. Therefore, true social transformation is really, in this sense, the kingdom of God without us, or external to us.

The true nature of society is divine just as is our true nature's. Thus, true social transformation can occur outside the full divine transformation of every person in society. This divineness is fixed and unchanging, but it is our progress to this, individually and collectively that is dynamic and changing into the unchangeable.

We look at society now as a verb in this context that it is changing and dynamic we see that "societing" is a movement towards something more full and complete. Thus, what is society but a collective expression of our own intents to something higher. It is the shared reason for interaction. To nurture itself as the nurturers within it nurture each other changes and upgrades its nature continuously until we are infinitely close to the nature we are to become, and in one sense we already are.

In one sense, society does have a mind of its own, and social movements are merely collective individual movements all united in one cause. The individual's external actions that make these movements observable to the outside world come from the inward world of unobservable movements that happen internal to the actor.

If society was to be considered an actor in itself, the internal movement it would have would be what we, as individual human actors today, call a social movement. The external movement of a society is and might be something we have never seen before on a complete scale, but has occurred and does occur among smaller subsets of society when subsocieties interact with subsocieties.

When individuals interact with each other, a social phenomenon emerges. When societies interact with each other it is a different and higher level of social phenomena. It's still a one on one interaction, though each one represents a community of variable sizes.

With this understanding, a social transformation can occur between only two people because that is all it takes to have a social encounter. But, true social transformation in the context of this book means a transformation of all the societies that make up the whole bigger society of the world. When looking at the world though as a society and subject to the same laws that apply to an individual, then really what is required is one big personal transformation, because there is only one society, which is the world.

However, just as one's personal mission is complete at 99%, neither could the world's transformation be complete if only 99% of the world's population transformed themselves. And, if we are to reach the status of 100% true sustainable change, then we need 100% participation.

Chapter 5

True Progress— What It Is and Is Not

In Chapter 1, we discussed the why of *why* as we questioned what purpose the question *why* serves. We said it is appropriate and expedient to ask why when trying to understand why your actions are no longer serving you.

Asking why, allows you to dive into the assumptions that could potentially be holding you back. This is why we started this book and this part of the book with expounding upon the doctrine of why. We are diving into the assumptions because many of our actions that go toward social transformation are not yielding any true and lasting results. We are both questioning why this is and giving an answer as to what the solution could be and why it is potentially the only true solution.

Social transformation can only occur through collective personal transformations is our main argument in this book, and in this chapter specifically we will discuss why we had to ask why and give a new solution due to the lack of progress our current actions are giving us.

It is interesting to look at progress in terms of both the hard sciences and the soft sciences. In the hard sciences such as math, science, and technology we have as of late made tremendous progress. In fact, we are progressing in this realm at an exponential rate.

However, in the soft sciences or the human sciences, we do not see this same progression of exponential growth and development. One reason could be that it is hard to measure, but another reason could be that all the measurement we are doing of ourselves is what makes it hard to progress in the first place.

The hard or natural sciences should be studied and dealt with in a way that is different than the soft or human sciences should be. When we try to study them both the same we objectify humans and humanize objects. Though as humans we do need to be dehumanized, but not into objects but into something more divine than humans.

The scientific method, which emerged from the modernist project to rationally reconstruct the world through science and an ever-progressing quest toward more freedom and control, has given us more and better objects, but unintentionally has made us, as humans, into objects in the process. If anything, this is the opposite of progress, but humans are resilient and have bounced back and pushed against the hegemonic force of science and in a way this has freed us because now we know what we are not. Yet, we still have much room to grow in the positive direction in terms of knowing what we are.

The whole idea of true social transformation hinges on us knowing who we are as humans, because the social world builds upon these truths and perceptions. If there was no difference between truth and perception we would arrive as people to the state of being completely transformed, but it is the problem of the soft sciences that has not been able to yield these universal truths about humans.

In the social sciences, the methods of the natural sciences were adopted to try and fix this pluralistic problem of relative perceptions by prescribing one method that would lead to the one truth. They were critical of the multiplicity of theories used to describe one social phenomenon, but ended up becoming what they despised in that they now use a multiplicity of methods. We are no closer than we were when science started its quest into the human realm.

This lack of progress in the social world or the human realm is what led us to ask how and where does true progress come from or how does a society evolve in the metaphysical or immaterial realm? Science can't provide these answers, though it tries so hard to, but maybe religion can?

Science has become a religion in a way and religion seems to be the most pluralistic field of study one could enter into. But, if we were to take truth as our religion and unify ourselves in that quest, we would find that maybe we all are essentially on one quest. One quest that is not pluralistic, but universal and shared by all. This would be the quest of personal transformation.

Many things can have the appearance of progress, but if they are not truly sustainable they are not true progress. It has been said that technology does not change anything, but can only accelerate whatever change is taking place.

Therefore, change does not come from objects or instruments of change, but from the agents of change who use these objects and instruments for change. Yet, even when they use the instruments, they do not create change with them, but use them to help to create the environment for change to occur. These objects and instruments make the choice to change easier by changing the environment.

Though, the changing environment is not true progress. It is the change in the people changing the environment wherein true progress is found. Therefore, all true social transformation occurs through the personal transformations of the people who are using the power of choice to choose to change the worlds they live in.

True social transformation is an inward change. The external changing of the environment is merely a fruit of the inward change. In our modern world today we are changing the external world and so we think that our inward world must be changing, but in what direction? If external change is the fruit of internal change, then all of this external change that is happening with the progress of society must be coming from something internal.

In the next part, Part II, we will define the "what" of change in terms of what is good change and what is bad change, because obviously society could transform itself into something that is 100% completely evil. Thus, enters ethics into the equation.

But here, we still remain on the why of our proposition and we see in this chapter that the reason why we had to ask the question that led to our main argument is because we have seen little, to none, to possibly backwards amounts of progress in the human and social sciences. Thus, we turn to a common religious quest.

Chapter 6

Society's Weakest Link(s)

Is a society only as strong as its weakest link? When we talk about the necessity of complete collective personal transformations as a prerequisite for true social transformation does that mean that one person can ruin it for all? Possibly, but only if those who are transformed allow them to. And, if they are truly transformed then they will choose not to respond to the person who has chosen not to be transformed.

This is how homogeneous societies used to sanction members for deviance and that they would shun them for misbehavior. This can often be the worst type of punishment. And, if someone is shunned by their society, they no longer are part of the society, and therefore the social transformation can still be complete without them.

In fact, in most cases the person will end up shunning themselves and separating themselves from the social group. These people should be allowed not to participate. Any desire from them to participate is a sign that they are not yet ready to be shunned or let go. They only become a lost cause when they no longer have any desire to interact with anyone.

Sometimes the lost can become lost together and then they create a lost society. Therein, the whole society is not whole because some have broken off and banded together apart from the rest. True social transformation would always include the whole of society. But, it can qualify as the whole of society if the whole part of society is willing to interact with everyone even if those who choose not to interact are not willing.

The willingness of the greater part is a sign of their full and complete personal transformations and the lost are no longer numbered among the members of the society. Therefore, in one sense the only people included in the count of a given society are those who are "societing" or doing the verb of society.

So, does majority rule? Like we talked about at the end of the last chapter, there are two directions for transformation to go in it is the transformation that includes the willingness to include even the unwilling are the ones who are transformed in the positive direction.

This does not need to be the majority to be considered the true society. It is because these people are the ones who are truly "societing" and their openness to socialize with all. The people transformed in the negative direction or the "lost causes" who have no desire to interact with the whole of society or at least the positively transformed members are not unconditionally "societing."

To be selective is not true "societing." It is conditional and a mark of either an untransformed person or a completely transformed person in the negative direction.

Therefore, true social transformation will occur at the point when everyone is transformed personally no matter what the direction they be in. C. S. Lewis said the world would end when all were either redeemed or unredeemable. This can be equated to when all are transformed either in the positive or the negative direction.

By pushing for the positive direction of transformations, those who are negatively oriented will transform themselves further and further into the negative stimulated by our pushing, until they arrive at their full and complete negative transformation.

The push towards the positive is essential in bringing out these transformations. Our main focus is full transformations. The Bible says better to be hot or cold than lukewarm (Revelation 3:16). Hot being positive, cold being negative, but either extreme is fully transformed. Social transformation is the end and every person's personal transformation is the means to that end. Though, they can also be seen as an end in themselves, by themselves.

The weakest links are the ones who are the fence sitters. The fully transformed negative people are very strong links even if they are in the negative. As time passes the weakest links will get weaker. Not in the sense of becoming even more lukewarm, but becoming or choosing their sides more definitively. When weaknesses get weaker they are really getting stronger. Therefore, when we say a society is only as strong as its weakest link we are saying more of the strength of the disparity between the positive verse the negative transformed people.

In the end, everyone will be transformed personally and true transformation socially will have occurred. But, only those transformed in the positive will be counted in the tally of the social transformation because it is impossible to have the "true" essence of social relations in a negative transformation pseudo-society. Those personally transformed themselves in the negative direction will be alone even if they are together. The negatively transformed will fall back down to complete dependence while the positively transformed will rise to inter-independent.

Independence and interdependence are closest on the two sides of lukewarm. These are the levels of those who are the weakest links and will become strong eventually. Though, the choice is theirs as to what direction they will strongly link with.

Chapter 7

Social Transformation— An Achievement or a Condition?

If the question ever came up on an exam whether or not social transformation or the ideal society was an achievement or a condition, the answers could be as various as different combinations would allow. It could be looked at as an achievement or as a condition alone. It could be looked at as both an achievement and a condition together. It can be looked at as neither an achievement nor a condition. And, it could be looked at as both both and neither and neither neither nor both.

This is a common form of logic that can be used in all forms of comparisons between dichotomies. Where's the truth within each of them?

Social transformation as an achievement

This one is probably the most easy of the ideas to wrap one's mind around. This follows a standard procedure of growth and development until you reach the point wherein growth and development is no longer possible. This point is usually called perfection or completion. It is the 100% of which we referred to earlier. This assumes that we must have started at zero and are inching our way upward closer and closer to 100%. Ideally, of course.

However, sometimes in history we get stuck and fluctuate around the same percentage for some time or even regress and go lower. Idealists, especially of the German tradition such as George Hegel and even Karl Marx see this progression towards the perfect society no matter what the appearance of regression is.

For example, Karl Marx thought though capitalism was evil it was what would ultimately through its fall bring about the ideal state of communism. Yes, it's how you look at it over the long term or the short-term. Maybe it's like the stock market and some days it seems like we're not achieving much, but if you look at it from the long-term perspective it's bound to make progress.

Social transformation as a condition

The word *transformation* seems to imply achievement as we talked about above, but what if there was no transformation from bad to good necessary? What if we were already good and all of our seemingly bad actions were just us not living true to who we are? What is the perfect society already is embedded within each of us and all of us both individually and collectively. Maybe it's just that we have forgotten what it looks like?

Perfection as a condition involves more of remembering what we already know versus learning something new. There is nothing to change, but merely become more and more of what you already are.

Though in one aspect, if you are not living according to who you already are then you would need to change, but the change would not be changing into something new but changing back into something old. And maybe because it has been so long since this old and ageless condition of mankind has been experienced it might seem new, but in reality it's who we have always been.

Social transformation as both an achievement and a condition

Now we get to try to combine both of these ideas. In a sense when you are who you are that is an achievement. Some people look at the quest for authenticity to be one of the greatest pursuits in this life. To find it is to become enlightened.

However, it is to be found by nothing that one already didn't have in their possession. It is not found externally, but internally. If it was already inside of us then it seems to be a condition that could be said to be shared among all. Therefore, what is being achieved has already been won.

Now, on the flipside, achieving itself can be part of our human condition. Maybe it's inherent within all of us to achieve something or at least the want to achieve. The coming to who one already is can be labeled as this achievement and can sometimes look like the linear model of progress we examined above. To blend both of these ideas we cannot say that on the path to achievement you are obtaining anything you didn't already have, but we can say that you are achieving something you have not yet realized yet in the external world.

All the seeds of every attribute, success, and achievement are already within you. Though they are a condition of you, their sprouting and maturing are up to you and the completion of the process will always bear its fruit.

Social transformation is neither an achievement nor a condition

Now how can we go back on everything we just said? If it's not an achievement nor condition than what could it be? In considering this, one must suspend all previous knowledge on the matter in relation between achievement and conditions in order to see what other possibilities there are.

On one hand, what it is already is and on the other hand what it is is not yet. And then, what it is already is and is not. But, here maybe the reverse would be what it is not already is and is not. This new polarity switches the negative to the first two words social transformation instead of playing with the order and classification of the other two words achievement and condition.

Does it simply imply a negative social transformation like we have talked about in previous chapters? Or, is this something completely new and different? Is this the no transformation idea wherein a person is a fence sitter and lukewarm? What does no transformation look like and how does it differ from negative transformation?

Negative transformation is as we talked about earlier and transforming yourself out of the possibility of being a social being and losing all the capacities of being human. Maybe no transformation is having all these capacities, but not exercising them wherein when you transform to the negative you lose them because you act in a way contrary to their positive transforming tendencies. Therefore, maybe no transformation is as we supposed being lukewarm and a fence sitter while negative transformation is being cold and of course positive transformation is being hot.

This brings up a good point though within the conversation. When there is no transformation occurring you are not achieving anything obviously but neither are you acting according to who you are and therefore you are not that anymore. Maybe you only are what you are when you are what you are? Negative transformation would be being who you are not, and no transformation would be not being at all. This leads us to think of Shakespeare's famous question, "to be or not to be?"

Social transformation is both both and neither, and neither neither nor both

How could something be both both and neither? It all depends on the person. How could something be neither neither nor both? It all depends on the person. Could someone be both both and neither and neither neither nor both at the same time? Yes, it is possible but it depends on the person.

When we say it depends on the person we mean to look at the phenomenon in a way that you look at every person differently and not generalize everyone. But further, we also mean that you look at all the different parts of one person differently and not generalize specific parts of them in an attempt to define them easier. And, you could go deeper by examining the parts within the parts of a person.

Now, going bigger, you could look at a society as one micro society or you could look at the macro society of earth and consider all the people and parts of a society. Then, you could look at our earth and its position in the society of the universe. Whether or not there are other forms of life out there? We seem to exist independent of our knowledge of them, but maybe it would be impossible to exist independent of their reality?

All questions between distinctions and the unfolding paradoxes can be examined indefinitely into depths so small and heights so tall while we attempt to understand the parts of life that are not too high to reach or too low to stoop to. Yet, it is in the ever ascending and forever descending that we both learn to fly and learn to sink. We never find an end as we go upward and as we go inward the thing we find is the finding thing, which is not a thing at all.

Neither at the top do we find a thing, but more like the thing in us we find a being. Something that is as old and ageless as our common condition. Something that is achieving and ever transforming. Something that is both perfect but still progressing. Something that embodies every paradox and possible perspective while still only yielding one truth. That something is not the one sum of everything added together, but is someone adding together everything.

So, is social transformation or the perfect society an achievement? Yes. A condition? Yes. Both? Yes. Neither? Yes. Okay, so is social transformation or the perfect society an achievement? No. A condition? No. Both? No. Neither? No.

Maybe this is why our communication should be no more than "yea, yea and nay, nay. Whatsoever is more than this cometh of evil" (Matthew 5:37).

We would say whatsoever is less does also. When we try to look at the world too simply, we lose so much. When we try to overcomplicated we win so little. When we do it right we win so much more, lose so much less.

All of this talk is transferable to the same transformational principles which apply to persons. Our own process as individuals follows the same rules and logic as which applies to collective transformations. But, if it is the same and we are using this positive/negative logic then it is also probably different.

But, different how? It all comes down to what society is. A society can act like a person, but is ultimately not a person. It does not act on its own, but people act through it and it through people. The conditions and achievements of society spring up and spring into the people as they spring up from their actionless state of merely existing and spring into action through their choices and their choices' consequences.

Society is nothing of itself, and can therefore not achieve anything on its own nor is anything of its own merit. It merits and does its existence to persons who don't just exist but act and engage in social interaction. It is the voluntary acts of individuals (plural) that when both given and received between each other is personal phenomena transformed to social phenomena.

Therefore we have another transformation. Personal actions are transformed into social actions. Therefore, personal transformations can be transformed into a social transformation. And thus, we both support and add to the main argument of this book.

Not only can social transformation only occur through collective personal transformations, but the word through is descriptive of another transformational process which occurs. Therefore, we could even venture to say that personal transformations transform into social transformation.

That has a little bit different of a ring to it. The transformation of one person is literally taking a different form as a social phenomenon instead of only a personal process.

Chapter 8

Personal Transformation into Social Beings

Part of our transformation as persons involves becoming more than just a person, but becoming part of a bigger group of persons and taking on the plural of the word person.

A person becomes part of a people. People are persons and persons are people. A person can never be so different that he could not be classified to any group of people. If he could, then he probably shouldn't be classified as a person in the first place.

The one thing all humans have in common is that we all have at least one thing in common. This is the starting point for the possibility of the move from being a single person to being part of the plural of people. In order for true and unified social transformation to occur, all people must share the undergoing of their own personal transformations, because a social transformation is really a transformation of people (plural) and therefore we are almost redundant when we say social trans-formation through collective personal transformations, because that is the only possibility.

They are one and the same. Though, when we state it so simply it helps to orient our minds to focus on the simple truth. You can't transform a group of people more than each person within that group will allow themselves to be transformed.

Related to our conversation on inter-independence, nothing can force us to become social beings. Most of us choose it not because of some outward law, but because of some inward orientation to the social. We both desire to extend ourselves and reach from within outward to the social world and also intend for others in that social world to reach out and into our own lives. It is part of our personal being to also be social. Our social self also has a person, which we call a personality. It is this interplay between our personal self and our social self that we engage within social processes before we even engage with other social beings.

Yet, ironically we wonder if we cannot engage with the social process without having ever engaged with it previously. We look here sometimes we see ourselves as others see us. We think this is looking at ourselves through the lens of society, though it is really our own personal lens shaped by us according to the social factors that we let shape us. Therefore, we can engage with a social process without even being social.

But, is it a prerequisite to have had some social experience to go through this social process on our own?

We believe it is. It is because we can bring out new things and ideas from within us that we can also project what new reactions in society these new creations of ours would stimulate. Having never seen these reactions, we can also create what we think they would be.

Therefore, we are in a sense creating society before we even experience it. What would happen if we were to experience it and then create it?

This is what we have also talked about earlier as the human capacity to choose your response to external stimulus. In looking at society as an external component we realize that it also probably has an internal component.

The internal component is the social being--who you are, what you are--not being social. When you choose your response you are acting from within. You are being the social being you create instead of the social being that reacts. The reacting social being is really not a being at all, but a thing. Therefore, because you are not a thing you are not being truly social when you act like a thing.

Thus, true social interaction comes only from social beings that interact first inwardly as social beings and then subsequently their "beingness" is transformed into a truly external social phenomenon. Therefore, a social transformation must first occur within every person before it occurs without or external for every person.

Our first task is to transform the social nature within us and by doing so we also complete the second task.

C. S. Lewis once said, "Put first things first and we get second tings thrown in: put second things first and we lose *both* first and second things." Therefore, external social transformation is the second thing that we must not put first. We must first transform the social being within each person.

As we do so, we will have a people who are truly socially transformed and can live in a truly transformed society. A person who has not undergone this transformation or who underwent a transformation contrary to that of the society in which he hopes to be a part can never engage truly with that society unless he was transformed with that society.

The social transformation we see here is and can be classified under the same category as the personal transformations we referred to in the main thesis or argument. The true social transformation of which we refer to in the argument or in the title of this book, is the external social transformation.

We refer to this type of social transformation because it is the one that most people think of and is the one that would be observable to the outside world. Though, those who are truly socially transformed inwardly do not need to see any external validation for their social transformation, but for us as yet to be transformed social beings we see and hold this as our ideal in hopes to understand better the process that will make the ideal not only possible, but real.

We will realize the ideal when we idealize reality. If we do not start living as a people first as persons we will not as persons be able to live as a people. Each person must become a people in theirselves if we are to become a people in ourselves.

Chapter 9

The *True* and *Only* Way to Change the World

In this part, and throughout the previous eight chapters we have sought to expound upon our central argument of why true social transformation can only occur through collective personal transformations. We examined the word *true*, we looked at what type of social transformation we are referring to (external), and we hopefully made both enough sense and an impression as to why this is true.

It is a bold claim to use the word *true* and *only* in an argument, but we believe that if this is true it is the only way to look at the idea and problem of social transformation. Therefore, *true* and *only* always must go together. So must *true* and *always* only go together. We could say that true social transformation always occurs through collective personal transformations and this gives a different light in which we can see the truth a little brighter.

We can even say that social transformation is always dependent upon personal transformations and this statement gives no orientation to the direction of the transformation, whether it be positive or negative. Thus, we also concluded that in speaking of transformation we imply that this transformation be toward the positive and, the positive is what we assume to be as true.

In the next chapter, we will describe more of what the positive looks like. In talking of transformation, one cannot not talk of ethics.

One cannot describe an ideal without prescribing practices that lead to that ideal.

We cannot separate the ideal of this book from the reality of its acceptance. We hope and can say it would be ideal if everyone believed as we believed and saw why we say why we say what we say in the same light, but we also know that people can see why we say what we say without believing what we say. They are free to come up with their own why as to how they believe social transformation or rather true social transformation does or can occur. In that statement we are expressing a *how*, and in this chapter we have been trying to give the *why* to how this *how* is true.

We have sought to answer why our claim that it is only through collective personal transformations that any true social transformation could ever be possible. We have discussed the possibility of probability of this being right. It is either absolutely true or not worth considering. Its merit does not even lead to the possibility of it being false and therefore we must assume that it is impossible for it not to be true.

Therefore, we continue to hold to our claim and say with surety that we know it to be true that true social transformation can only occur through collective personal transformations. And, not only can it only occur in this way, but that it only does occur in this way. And, that it only has occurred in this way and will only ever occur in this way.

Truth is as things were, are and are to come and therefore we believe this to be true.

In the next part and proceeding chapters, we will look further into trueness and what we believe it to be. Truthfulness cannot be separated from its implications and therefore as we discover the truth we uncover our untruthfulness. As we see with greater light, we see the black spots of our own inadequacy that have been hidden by darkness.

These black spots are anything that go contrary to the argument. If this argument is true, then any other comparable argument cannot be true. It cannot stand alone, though it can stand with the truth of this truth.

We will look into and discover these truths further as we seek further to establish this truth. The reader will see without the writer having to point out all the ways in which they the reader try to do what the writer says not to do. Without saying what to do or what not to do, the reader can know what or what not to do.

We proclaim only what we believe to be true and we let anything that is not true take itself out of commission. We do not force it out of commission in risk of committing an act not in alignment with our commission to only communicate the truth.

With this being said, we do not suppose that we are above any other supposition of man, but can conclude that we are being conclusive in our argument. What person along us would want to hear anything that is not conclusive or succinct. We are therefore then successful in this way by being succinct. Even if we are wrong, we are not wrong to conclude what we believe to be true.

We are not wrong to assume what we presume to be true. It is better for a man to believe with all his heart something that is wrong than to halfheartedly believe that which he thinks might be right but is unsure of. One is more right to believe fully in the wrong than to not believe fully in the right. If we believe we are right, we will act more rightly than the man who believes all are wrong including himself.

We can thus then assert with a surety that we are sure what we assert in that true social transformation can only occur through collective personal transformations. There is no other way, there is no other choice, and there is no other truth. We used the word *only* because we are claiming a monopoly on the ways, choices, and truths around the concept, ideal, and efforts toward true social transformation.

We not only see that our quest is still incomplete here in terms of describing and prescribing the how and the what of these two inseparable transformations, but we also observe that any completeness of the ideas above can be completed by those with ideas that go above and beyond these already stated. We seek only to set some part of the first foundation upon which framers more wise and intelligent than us can build a framework that will work to hold up the expansive building of truth that seems as high of an ideal as does the idea of infinite expansion.

What if one foundation could hold all that ever was, all that ever is, in all that ever will be? This would be quite sturdy to build upon. It would be solid enough at least for one person to stand, but if it was what it claimed to be then it would be strong enough to hold all.

It is to all that we hope this claim to be considered by and to all we hope to stand with on the foundational idea that true social transformation can only occur through collective personal transformations.

II

We then go on to elaborate
some of the core philosophies that
make these transformations possible
as well as suggest to
what end these transformations be
directed

Chapter 10

The *Why* of This *Why*— Core Philosophies

Just like we started the first part of the book with a discussion on the concept of *why*, we will start this part of this part, Part II, with a discussion about why we are now discussing what this part is about.

In this part, we will elaborate upon some of the core philosophies that make transformations possible. We will state our assumptions and beliefs and try to give reasons for why we assume what we assume and believe what we believe.

As we discussed these core beliefs, out of them will arise many implications for actions that one should take if they were to believe as we believe. These implications are prescriptive in nature and thus should or ought to be put in practice immediately.

Why would it be foolish to continue onward after discussing why true social transformation can only occur through collective personal transformation to tell about how these transformations actually take place?

Jumping too quickly from *why* to *how* without explaining all of the cultural and ethical assumptions that go into the how would be like trying to describe something green to someone who is colorblind. If you use green as a descriptive word, you are assuming that they have experienced greenness before and can thus relate to what you are saying.

It is for that reason that we find it necessary to our task at hand to spend this next part of the book explaining some of the core philosophies we have in order for you the reader to be able to relate better to these ideas and thus experience with us their truthfulness and their potential power to transform the way and the what of what we are to transform into.

For example, if we believed that the ideal human being was someone animalistic by nature, we would suggest that transformation into animalhood be honored and enacted by the masses of society. It is important to have faith, but it is also important to know what your faith is in. To just transform for the sake of transforming would be futile unless you happened to get lucky and by mistake end up transforming into something that we would here suggest needs to be intentional.

The possibilities are endless as to what one could transform themselves into, but here we prescribe one possibility which includes all others, but is not limited by the illusion of limitless possibilities.

There can every time be infinite possibilities, but also at every time it is which possibility to choose that leads to the next set of infinite possibilities. And, though it is strange to think about the infinite possibilities that come from the choice from the last possibility you chose, sometimes, they do not include the same possibilities as the last choice you had.

But, how can something infinite not include everything? It is the advancement from possibility to possibility that we see to the end of our first possibility. If we do not have any direction to go any choice that is presented could possibly be the best choice, but once we have a direction that we want to go there is only one possibility.

This possibility always exists. Even when the direction seems impossible to pursue, possibility will still always emerge as long as one believes it is possible. "If thou canst believe all things are possible to him that believeth" (Mark 9:23).

This is why in this part of the book we want to lay out some of the core beliefs that we ask people to believe in. If hard at first, it is sometimes best first to suspend all previous beliefs and allow yourself to consider the possibility of what we are proposing to be true. You might find that as you do, this belief will work within you until you find a possible way that it could actually be true and fit into what you already believe.

In essence, we are prescribing ways to believe and ways to see the world because these ways are imperative for the possibility of this world being transformed in a way that is full, true, and complete. We are giving the ideal of what we are to become.

In the next chapter we will seek to show the process, but here we give the outcome. Through goals we transform faith into action through an intentional process toward these goals we can achieve transformation or return and transform back to our already perfect condition. However you want to look at it.

We are seeking to construct the theoretical framework in which the rest of the book can have context within. We laid the foundation for why and now recommence to further the building of the structure by continuing our discussion from the above stated perspective and for the above stated reasons.

Much of these ideas are not common thinking, but this is why we think we have an uncommon monopoly on the ideas that can actually transform the world. Albert Einstein once said, "The significant problems we face today cannot be solved at the same level of thinking we were at when we created them."

We develop some of these ideas to think about the world and how to best help it. We do not claim to have all the ideas, but claim to have enough to get started moving in the right direction. Enough to know that there is a direction that is more right than others. The right direction being that social transformation can only occur through personal transformations, but also knowing to what and these transformations be directed is part of the direction too.

How we see the world is how the world is for us and if we change the way we look at things we change the things we look at. Let's begin!

Chapter 11

The Different Way of Thinking—Eternity, Infinity, and Spirituality

Continuing from the quote at the end of the previous chapter by Albert Einstein, we will now commence first with our foundational way of thinking about thinking. For our way of thinking, all that is not eternal is too short. All that is not infinite is too small. All that is not spiritual is too insignificant. This approach to thinking about matters is integral throughout all of our core concepts.

For example, in terms of helping the poor we often hear the saying give a man a fish feed him for a day, but teach a man to fish feed him for a lifetime. This is a little bit closer to infinity, but we like to take it one step further. If you could teach a man to teach men how to fish you could feed many men for a lifetime and if you could teach a man how to teach men to teach men how to fish, you could feed that for their lifetime and for generations to come. This is both eternal and infinite and spiritual in perspective.

It is infinite in that a man can now feed more than just himself through feeding people through proper education. It is eternal in that his influence extends beyond his own lifetime and proceeds to all of his descendants and all of the descendants of those he influenced. It is spiritual in the sense of what is being conveyed toward the end.

To teach how to teach is one of the most spiritual journeys one could ever take. To truly teach is to not teach it all, and thus to truly teach how to teach takes a lot of spiritual maturity. It is because the man is not the teacher, but the spirit that is in and between and through all things including them.

When this type of teaching occurs it is not to give information, but provide a space for transformation. Thus, both the teacher and the learner are transformed together as true teaching occurs. These transformations are eternal in duration and can be infinite in scope. Thus, all spiritual, eternal, and infinite components to the equation are interwoven as are most triads.

Why do we use eternity, infinity, and spirituality? Philosophers have long said that reality can be broken down into three main components: time, space, and matter. These are the realities for our world, but the high level of thinking are realities of the higher world or the higher realm.

The higher realm is the realm of the transformed. It is the higher world in which we are striving toward in which we have already within us. Time correlates to eternal, space is infinite, and spirit is actually a form of matter just more fine and not visible to the common eye. Spirit is light, and when we think of it like that, we realize there is only a small part of the spectrum of light that is actually visible. Spiritual matter cannot be measured by material means, but is only known through spiritual methods. It is these methods that religions prescribed toward spiritual enlightenment and rebirth.

When considering eternity, infinity, and spirituality, it is almost impossible to stay away from the realm of religion. We think that staying away from this realm is one of the most core problems of all problems. At the root of every cause we think we have identified, is a cause that is more "root-a-mentory", and that cause is a spiritual one.

Both societal and personal ills are spiritual in nature. A society crumbles quickest when its spiritual immune system is weak and the same goes with a person. There is both a mind and body connection and a spirit and mind connection. And, thus a spirit and body connection. The mind mediates the conversation between the outside world that is experienced through the senses and the inside world of the spirit.

The spirit can be a sense just as powerful or more powerful than the five common physical senses. You will find that it always makes the most sense to listen to this sense, but is only appreciated as such after the fact. It is often what we call maybe common sense or intuition, but maybe it's a sort of common light we have all been given as humans?

This light, however, does not control us unless we allow it to. It is as bright as we allow it to be.

Thus, some people who do not let their light shine can be in internal darkness. For them, their external world can seem dark too and thus they seek for other ways to lighten their lives. But, these ways are as temporary as are the temporal and physical world in which they belonged to and which they use to alleviate their disease of darkness. Enduring light and fulfillment can only come from within and it is inside of us that we find the part of us that is infinite, eternal, and spiritual.

At the innermost part of society, we find the same infinite, eternal, and spiritual truth, because the innermost part of society is its members. And, its members are us. And, we are infinite, eternal, and spiritual. Thus, a society that does not listen to spiritual things is at the risk of the same darkness of a person that doesn't listen to spiritual things or allow their light to shine.

As a society, we will look for things external to save us such as the law, the makers of the law, or the enforcers of the law. However, the salvation is likewise always as temporary as the temporalness of which it is constituted.

When one starts seeing the world from an eternal perspective one can see that each moment is part of eternity. Each moment has an eternal shortness just as we can more easily comprehend how eternity has its longest.

It is the same with infinity. The world external to us is endlessly big as the world internal to us is endlessly small. Spiritual matter and spiritual matters have the greatest impact because they make an impact at such a deep and primary level.

A plane starting off 1° in the wrong direction will eventually find itself thousands of miles off course. When we are misaligned spiritually, because all things spring out from the spirit it is our starting point and any degree of misalignment can impact our journey significantly.

This is only the beginning of one of the ways to think about the world which includes in itself three distinct ways to look at the world. This trinity of perspectives is what will allow you the reader and we the writers to be transformed the instant we transform our minds into thinking in this way. "Be ye renewed by the renewing of your mind" (Romans 12:2).

Chapter 12

Ontology of Humans

The next two chapters could potentially be combined in that they go hand-in-hand in the process of the claim to truth. Ontology asks the question "what is it" and epistemology asks "how do you know". Ontology tries to describe what an object or phenomenon is while epistemology describes the method used to come to that knowledge.

In this chapter, we will discuss the ontology of humans or what humans are. This is so fundamental for understanding anything else we say in regards to social realities, because how you understand humans is how you see society and how you structure society.

For example, in the Western world, one ideology has reigned since before it was even stated. Saying that it existed before there were symbols to adequately express what it is implies that we believe it to be accurate. We both do and we don't. Let us explain.

The idea that humans are self-interested beings was one most chiefly held by Thomas Hobbes, a prominent English philosopher of the 1600s. He and others have shared this claim that we as humans are fundamentally self-interested.

There are two lines of thought when it comes to this self-interest. One is psychological egoism which states that we *can only* act out of our own self interest. The other is ethical egoism which says that we *should* act only out of our own self interest. Not all ethical egoists are psychological egoists. And, it doesn't make sense for a psychological egoist to believe the ethical part because would it truly be ethical to do something you *ought* to do when it is the *only* thing you possibly *could* do?

Suggesting that we always act out of our own self interest is an ideology that is deterministic, behavioristic, and causal. It denies humans their full scope of agency and or voluntary action. If we could only be and act out of our own self interest then we would always be calculating our choices based on what option would yield the best outcome for us.

This calculative approach is comparative to how a computer computes. Maybe our minds can work like a computer, but maybe the bigger question is do we control our computers or do our computers control us?

This is the basic question at the root of this argument. What is the full extent of our human capacity to act? We can either act on our environment or react *to* our environment, and reacting is really the environment acting upon you. One who is in a predetermined self-interested mentality would always be reacting to situations attempting to respond in the way that best suited his needs and wants.

Now, this does not say that we cannot choose to voluntarily act in ways that are for our own best interest, nor that we should not not ever act in our own self interest, but that at the heart of what ever we do must be an understanding that whatever we do is and or can be a choice.

Prescribing all men to be one certain way says that there is no other way but that way. Prescribing that all men *should* be one way is different in that it doesn't limit people to the way, but invites them to live that way.

Therefore, psychological egoism is and can be thrown out as a valid theory in our book figuratively and in this book literally. Ethical egoism, on the other hand, is a different question. But, before we get into ethical egoism, let us first look at the possibility of altruism.

Possibility of Altruism

The possibility of altruism exists first in the truth of possibility itself. If we do have the freedom to choose then we technically could choose to act in a way contrary to our own self interest. The problem in knowing true altruism is the unobservableness of motives. It seems only the actor them self can know themselves and their true reasons for acting.

An act can have the appearance of self-interest, but really have been done for the interest of the other. And vice versa, an act can have the appearance of interest for the other, but really have been done out of the actor's own self-interest.

Thus, we cannot prove altruism empirically through our own observation and even if we were to ask the actor to describe the meanings of their actions we could still not conclude empirically, because they could obviously, or even worse *un*-obviously, be lying.

How we know true altruism outside of ourselves is a question more of epistemology, which we will get to, but to touch a little on it now there is an irony in knowing it. The irony is this: those who think altruism is impossible have probably not ever experienced it for themselves and those who know it's possible have only their own experience of it to base their belief. The person who sees the world as only self-interested probably acts only self-interestedly. The person who believes in altruism will and can act altruistically.

Are there people who only act altruistically? This would be psychological altruism. Maybe, though we cannot prove it. But, just because someone only acts that way we must remember that it is by choice and not by force of their very nature. A psychological altruist in the true sense would *only* be able to act out of others' interests.

This might sound absurd, but in reality it is probably just as absurd as the converse theory of psychological egoism.

Many religions proclaim an ethic of altruism and helping your neighbor, but also realize that one must respect themselves enough to take care of themselves too. And, that it is not in the rest of the world's interest for you to kill yourself trying to save everyone else, because when you are dead you cannot help as many people as when you are alive and well.

Thus, most people spend their lives balancing this dichotomy. Most often when young, we act mostly out of our own self interest until we earn enough resources to be able to "give back."

In terms of what is happening, this might be okay and might be rightly ethical by all means, but what we prescribe goes beyond and before both extreme viewpoints of both psychological egoism and psychological altruism. We suggest that one not merely balance between the two, but blend them both into one.

The Blend

We often think of self-interest as bad and other-interest as good, at least from a religious and moral perspective, and therefore if we want to be good all we have to do is flip our natural, "evil", selfish motives and act altruistically. But, we often find that extreme altruism is just as bad as extreme egoism. The blend we prescribe is that you need not flip your motives, but switch your perspective for your motives.

The perspective is this: when you see others as yourself and you see yourself as an other all are on equal ground. No person including you or even your neighbor is above or below each other. What is above both you and your neighbor is the higher power or God.

This viewpoint is very biblical in nature, but also very practical in its nature to. The Bible says that the greatest commandment is to "love the Lord thy God with all thy heart, and with all thy soul, and with all thy strength, and with all thy mind" (Luke 10:27). This love is and should be 100% completely on God, because of the qualifier *all*. Therefore, there is not one percent left for you or for your neighbor. Thus, you are equal in that you are both at zero.

This is different than loving your neighbor the same and trying to always walk a balance line of 50-50. 50% loving yourself and

50% loving your neighbor. This says 100% on God and 0% on you. But, there is more than this.

If you love God you will keep his commandments (John 14:15). One of his commandments is to love him and therefore when you love him you are commanded to love him and thus you love him more. This is infinite and perpetual love. But, the second is like unto it but that you love your neighbor too. "Inasmuch as ye have done it unto one of the least of these my brethren, ye have done it unto me" (Matthew 25:40). Therefore, you love God by loving each other. Remember that other includes you now, too.

A story from my personal life: I remember one time I did something and accused or determined the cause of my action to be something that I had learned from my brother. I told someone when explaining my reasons for acting the way I did that, "I was acting in the *spirit* of my brother."

When we act in the *spirit of God* we are acting from a place of unconditional love. From his perspective we are all others, and this is the perspective we must switch into. From this perspective we see things as he sees them and we see everyone, including ourselves, as one and the same.

With that said, it makes no difference whether someone acts out of self-interest or other-interest because the self is considered as an other and the other is considered as a self. God is a psychological egoist in that everything he does is in his own self interest and that by helping us he helps himself. But, He is also a psychological altruist in that He loves himself through loving us. Therefore, whatever he does is and has the same effect.

Now, tying in ethics to the equation. If it is ethical to act in either way, then we see that God is therefore perfect because whatever he does is ethical.

Thus we see that the ontology of human beings can be either one and should be either one. The question is, from what perspective should we perceive the world? This perspective is imperative to the ontology of human beings.

We seem to have two extreme natures. One, can become animalistic and the other can become divinistic. A human is one who operates from both sides. We had a nature that is natural that seems to be animalistic, egoistical, and fit the theories of reactive self-interest ontologies, but we also have a human nature that we can change into and become that it is possible to act out of others' interests and see as others see. The greatest other being from God's perspective.

Speaking of transformation in the context of this book, we see the need in order to transform ourselves into the divine nature which is a positive transformation instead of being transformed into the animal nature which would be a negative transformation.

Thus, like we have said before, the choice is ours and this choice is the most salient feature of our humanness. This choice is what lets us decide where to enter into the choiceless state.

When we choose to transform ourselves negatively, we become like an animal and lose control of ourselves. But, when we choose to transform ourselves positively into the divine state we give up our control, but find that we are given more control than we ever could have imagined before.

Therefore, in both we give up control, or our choice, but only in one we gain more than we could ever give. Negative transformation is infinitely close to zero and thus is equivalent to zero. Positive transformation can infinitely go on forever and more control will continue to be given to you as you give more and more of your control now over to the controller of all things, mainly God.

Chapter 13

Epistemology of Our Approach

Epistemology, as we said before, is how we know what we know. All of our claims above about the ontology or nature of human beings have come to us in certain ways.

There are three main ways to know truth. One can learn through the body, through the mind, or through the spirit. These three ways can correlate with more intellectual terms: empiricism, rationality, and intuition. In terms of all three of these, one is not better than the other, but there is an order to them.

We should submit our bodies to our minds and our minds to our spirits. We do this all the time through common life experiences. We often try to make sense with our minds with what the senses of our body tell us.

Rationality is acting logically. But, sometimes rationality can be irrational if what seems most logical does not seem to be congruent with our gut feeling. In these cases, we will often act irrationally according to our spirit. Though some people ignore this feeling and move forward anyway, we submit that it is best and is right to submit your perception of the external world to your senses and your rational mind to the intuitive influence of the Spirit. The spirit-led approach will always serve you better than any other approach no matter how tempting it might seem.

In the world today, we have this order mostly backwards. We rely so much on science, which is based in objectivity and empiricism. Empiricism like we said before is a complete sensory system of attaining truth. And objectivity, is a method for removing the human, and thus the human spirit, out of the experiment so it is not a variable. Seeking truth in this way is not evil in itself, but only when it is the only way.

With this mindset, everything must be validated. All assumptions must be tested. Proof, in some cases absolute proof, must be given before action is taken. However, there are some things that just cannot be proven through the senses.

In this sense, we need another method to find truth. Rationality is what is most used to handle truths or concepts that are more abstract that cannot be tested concretely.

With rationality, we can analyze and synthesize our observations in the facts posited by them. We can participate in a dialectic or debate of ideas in order to rationalize our way to the most logical and coherent truth available to mankind. We can sit and mentally work out any problem and suggest the solution that seems most logical.

Rationality is often linked with the idea of self-interest in the un-ideal form. But, as we stated in the last chapter, if and when rationality can be viewed from the perspective of God then it would have a new logic to work from.

Thus, like the mind, rationality in itself is merely a tool to sort through information that comes from the outside and also from the inside.

The information that comes from the inside is what we call intuition. It is what religions refer to as the spirit. Being led by the spirit, whether it be God's, yours, or a mix and blend of both, is the same in the sense that it comes from a source that is mostly self stimulated except for in occurrences of divine intervention.

The way truth comes from the outside is through stimulation and then is understood through the mind, but the way truth comes from the inside is through some sort of self stimulation that comes from within and can but does not necessarily need to go through the mind.

Just like one can act straight from the body without going through the mind, such as in cases where the reflexes are used and information goes from the nerves to the spinal cord and back to the nerves. The brain and or mind can be bypassed when operating from a completely spiritual perspective. Yet, just as is the case with the body that most actions do go to the mind, so is the case with the spirit. It is only in special circumstances that the mind is not utilized in the process of action.

Knowing that the spirit and body can operate independently of the mind is fundamental in under-standing the separateness of each component. It is fundamental in learning how to learn.

In terms of personal and social transformation, true transformations always include and are led by the spirit. It is one of the hallmarks of the modern age of science to seek progress through a body and mind approach only. With the separation of church and state, we have excluded spirit from body in the work of growth and development. Our schools are filled with facts and experiments, which is good, but without the spirit it can never be right.

Though we talk of the spirit, we need not to all be of the same religion to utilize the spirit. Not all scientists need to believe the same things in order to use empirical means for discovering truth. Just like every-*body* is different, so is every-*spirit*. Yet, though we are different, we also *are*, in terms of existing, for the same reason.

The scientist does their science to find truth just as the spiritualist uses the spirit to find truth. Without the spirit being involved in the process of transformation, we could never have true transformation. We could and are transforming at an exponentially rapid rate in terms of science, empiricism, and bodily pursuits of progress, but even if we reached the pinnacle of transformation in this realm, it would still be incomplete.

True transformation must involve the spirit. If we were to only do the spirit-side of transformation with as much intensity as we have done the body-side, we would not be complete. The spirit will never exclude the body from its progress, but the body does exclude the spirit from its, or at least it tries.

It's when the spirit is first that the body will inevitably come from it, but if we put the body first the spirit will go away from it.

Remember back to the quote about putting first things first and getting second things thrown in. Even though the body was created first and the spirit of man put in the body, we recognize that it was only created first to hold a place for the spirit. In our modern age we have created a body that is empty of the spirit and thus primed and ready to be filled and subsequently transformed in just as rapid a way as has been the history of science.

Chapter 14

Man's Ontology and God's Ontotheology

Man's potential ontology is God's current ontotheology. Ontology deals with the nature of being. Ontotheology deals with the nature of God's being. How connected are these and how possible is it for man to become like God?

The three adjectives we always use to describe God are omnipotent, omniscient, and omnipresent. Or, in other words he is all-powerful, all-knowing, and all-present.

We will examine these three components of deity and show how it is possible for man to transform himself in a way to become like deity Himself, and possibly sooner than you would expect.

Omnipotent

Is being all-powerful measured by capacity, history, or present reality? Capacity deals with potential. How much could one do? History deals with the past. How much has one done? Present reality deals with the now. How much is one doing?

Looking at power from the past and the future one relates to it directly. It is only when we look at power in the present that we can directly experience it.

One is being powerful when they are acting in a powerful way. But, a powerful being is powerful even if their actions aren't proving their power constantly. Though independent of acts of power, a powerful being is always being powerful. The proof of their power does not always manifest itself in the external world through empirical means, or through the mind, but often through the heart or the spirit. True power is something that you sense internally and that moves you internally.

Though God does have immense external power and he could exercise it in this way, he yields his power most directly through the truer means of internal exertion. Another way one could look at it is that God is both all-powerful and all-empowering.

He moves things forward in the external world through empowering the internal worlds of the movers. In this sense, we too can be like God when we empower people to act for themselves.

Acting independently is an attribute of deity and we are like God when we help others to be like God. God gods (verb) gods (us). And thus, when we god (verb) gods(others), we are being like God and acting in an all-powerful and all-empowering way.

Tied to the concept of allness is omniscience, because the all-powerful is being in some sense all things to all people. Though we often are critical of this idea, it has some truth in it. We can be all things to all people when we are one to one person. Then, if you synthesize the ideas of oneness and allness, can you also translate this divine aspiration to human perspiration acting diligently and wholeheartedly like divinity itself.

Omniscience

Same as there was with power, there are both direct and indirect ways of knowing. God, both through us and independent of us, knows things of us. We can know of things and of people in both of these ways.

As a leader, you can know the status of someone's well-being without actually knowing them by talking to their supervisor whom you supervise. This is an indirect way of knowing. With our weak human capacities to translate perfectly what we observe into what we communicate, we often reduce in some way the true nature of the phenomenon every time we interpret and explain, but as we share our ability to do this we become more like God. He doesn't lose anything. Nothing gets lost in translation.

The reason why this is and can be is because of his direct way of knowing. He is the one connecting with the object or person to be known. He, as the knower, can know even what the knowee doesn't know. He does this through a delicate process of discernment where he connects soul to soul with the person and/or object.

The knowee could give an accurate report of themselves, if they were to be connected with themselves congruently body, mind, and spirit. But, the spirit holds the key of knowledge of the rest of the body and therefore connected to this is like the USB portal to know the entire system.

We can connect spirit to spirit with people in the same way. We have the capacity to do so now just as God does it now. In this way, we can be all-knowing. Tapping into the spirit is tapping into the universal knowledge system of the universe and therefore you can know all things by knowing how to do this one thing. God connected to us is connected to all and we if connected to God can be connected to all and therefore be omniscient as well.

Omnipresent

Much like all other paradoxes, which God embodies, is that God can be everywhere, but nowhere at the same time by being in one place always. To be physically present is different than having a spiritual presence.

The spirit of something or someone can be somewhere without the someone or something being there. The Christmas spirit is merely the spirit of Christ. All things good come from God and all things evil come from the devil.

God is light and the devil is darkness. Darkness is not anything on its own, but the absence of light. Non-presence of God is therefore the absence of the presence of God. Can God be present where he is not? Can darkness be where there is not light? If there is not light, then there is darkness, but darkness in terms of reality fades away into non-reality and therefore wherever reality is so is God. And therefore, he can be everywhere where being is or does exist.

Can we be and do the same? Yes, in the same way that we be and do the same in terms of being all-powerful and all-knowing. When we transform ourselves into God, we become as he and his spirit is our spirit. His presence is our presence and therefore our presence is all-present.

Presence also denotes another meaning, and that is of time. All-present is being both everywhere and anywhere and being there every time and at any time. Because God is not anywhere but here, nor everywhere but there, we can assume he is both with you and I and us together and alone speaking of presence as a place alone.

Speaking though of his presence in time, we realize that time is a social construct. God lives outside of whatever limits we could ever try to put him in. For him, there is no past or future, but only the present. He lives from moment to moment just as we do, but unlike us he actually lives in the moment. Living in the moment is what gives him the momentum to be there for us in every moment.

It is in the moment that one taps into the present moment, that one discovers the all-being presence of God.

Chapter 15

Idealism and Realism

Why having a small vision is sometimes best

True social transformation can be comparable to the more common phrase, "to change the world" we hear all the time. People have an amazing idea and say with all hope and faith that it could change the world. To change the world seems to be one of the biggest visions one could hold in terms of what they hope they or their product or service could offer.

Having this big vision serves a purpose, but what would a smaller vision look like? And, could the smaller vision serve the same purpose?

This is the idea here. Instead of going out to change "the" world, one could also focus instead on going out to change "a" world. This focus on the indefinite article instead of the definite article can both switch our mindset and switch the course you take. In fact, it is only through the accumulation of the indefinite that one can possibly ever find the definite.

To find the truth, you start by looking for a truth. You find a truth here and you find one there and together you have a more definite picture of what the truth could be. The truth is all of the truths together. All of the truths separate are just a truths.

This is the same for social transformation as it is merely a collection of all the personal transformations. Therefore, having a vision to change a world is what will lead you to change the world.

Now, it could be tempting to start thinking that you need to not just change one world, but change many worlds. Thinking in this way is the same as thinking you need to change *the* world. It is often when you start small that you end big and when you start big you end small. But, if small is big and big is small than they are both great.

If you spend your whole life trying to change the entire world, but only change one person's life then your entire life's work is not in vain. If you spend your entire life trying to change one person, but they never change your life is still not in vain, because you yourself probably changed throughout.

People who change the world are often the ones who start with themselves and then move to helping those closest to them. This is an inside-out approach. Just like change must occur from the inside-out of an individual it must also occur this way on the social level too.

It has been said that we should think globally, but act locally. This is holding the dichotomy of both visions at once. You have a big vision to change the world, but you have a small vision and immediate application to change *a* world. And as Gandhi would suggest, the first world to change should be yours. This is, "being the change you wish to see in the world."

We often think that idealists think big and unrealistically and realists think small, practical, and even a bit unidealistically. However, what if the ideal was made practical through practicing reality in an ideal way? What if it was realistic to think that you could change the world?

People who know the correlation and trust the process of working by small and simple means to accomplish great things know that they can change *the* world by changing *a* world. In fact, every time you change a world you change the world in some way because that person you helped to change is part of the world. Changing the entire world population is changing the world's entire population.

Change has to occur one person at a time because change can only occur through the internal change of the individual. Thus, in order to change many people at once you make one invite to all for all to change themselves individually. But, though the effort and invite was extended to the collective, the change is accepted and implemented through the individual, because the change comes from within the individual.

When you go into an effort to change the collective you misunderstand that the change must occur through the individual. You can change by force or some imposed external law the collective, but this is only temporary. Permanent change only occurs one person at a time at the time the one person chooses to let it occur. This is the reality of the circumstances of change and therefore is also the ideal.

The ideal can match up with reality—and vice versa—if and when we understand that they are not two separate quests. If they are, some sort of misunder-standing has taken place and must be placed in its proper context if a pursuit towards the ideal is ever to take place and be really successful. *Really,* not being an adjective of emphasis, but of reality.

Real success is true success. Thus, reality can be the truth of the present and the ideal the truth of the potential. But, the potential isn't in the future but also in the present.

With this thinking, one can make the ideal real by realizing the ideal is not impracticable or in the future, but always present before us. One can change the world today by changing a world today. One could change the entire world today if the entire world changed today.

Therefore, we are always one choice away from the ideal and from true social transformation. One choice, speaking of the collective individual choices the world would need to make, but to focus on the choice a person, one person, needs to make is to see both the ideal and reality at the same time.

It can be just as hard to change one person as it is the world depending upon how stubborn the person is. The question is, how stubborn are we the world?

Chapter 16

Who Is a Change Maker?

There are many people who want the world to change.
There are some people who want to change the world.
Some of them will try,
but only few of them will succeed.

We cannot take up the question of who is a change maker without defining what true success is. In the above quote, it seems as if we are assuming that there is a difference between trying and succeeding. We believe that they are both is and is not.

Trying is not a success if no effort is tied to it. Thus, in this passive form of trying it is merely the same as those who passively want the world to change. Succeeding is wanting to change the world or is trying in its active form.

In this form, desire and action are synonymous. One who wants to change the world, does. *Does*, not in the sense that merely wanting will do it, but does as in they "do." He actually "does" something about it.

When action takes place so does some sort of change. Depending upon the orientation and direction of the action, the change can be positive or negative. People who merely try or just want the world to change are neutral.

This neutral apathy can actually be the worst type of negativity for those pursuing the positive, but for those pursuing the negative this type of apathy is positive, because in apathetic herd mentality, common followers are at the active change makers' disposal and it will be used as a means to their end.

Therefore, a change maker can be anyone who acts. But, a true change maker, in the positive sense, is one who acts sensibly in the positive direction. Because common sense isn't common, even those who are neutral tend to be change makers in the negative direction.

Change makers in the positive direction voluntarily choose that direction. Change makers in the negative direction voluntarily choose the negative direction. Those who just follow can never follow in the direction of the positive, because the positive is constituted by volunteerism or choice.

Therefore, they who do not pursue the positive will always be pulled down by and into the negative. It is the herd mentality that keeps us from the positive and it is the herd mentality that is most common. Because most of us never truly think for ourselves, we therefore never think of ourselves as changemakers.

With everyone being a change maker in some way, but only few being changemakers in the right way, *one of the first tasks of true changemakers is to help others become true changemakers.* This is done by first understanding what a change maker is, second recognizing what changes need to be made, and third making the changes.

The first change that needs to be made is that all people become change makers in the positive direction. This is the only way collective personal transformations can ever occur and thus how we have argued substantially in chapters before is the only way true social transformation can occur.

The direction in which these changes be made is the prescriptive and proscriptive portion of this part. It will include the next two chapters.

Chapter 17

A-ethical Ethics

We use the word *a-ethical* intentionally, because we believe that one's own personal ethical or moral code must be developed by the person them self. Aethical means without ethics. Unethical means acting contrary to ethics entirely. Thus, we are prescribing an ethic of non-ethics. But, as scary as that sounds we are also at the same time not prescribing an ethic of non-ethics.

The first ethic of non-ethics is the ethic of allowing all to choose their ethic. The second ethic of non-ethics that we are not prescribing is moral relativism meaning there be no ethic. No ethic is an ethic in itself.

We ethically claim that there should exist ethical claims which is an ethic in itself too. And, upon this assumption can we not justify any further than openly claiming that this is an assumption. This assumption obviously is grounded in many things, mostly of faith in God, but also in understanding basic laws of nature.

It goes back to our conversation about lightness and darkness. Darkness being the absence of light is the same as no ethics being the absence of ethics. We know that light is necessary for life and therefore we believe that ethics be necessary too. Unethical behavior is still light, but used for the wrong reasons. Therefore, at the core of all ethics is what is at the core of all behavior.

Outward actions are manifestations of inward decisions. Thus, our ethical code will deal with inward decisions and not outward manifestations of those decisions. We will focus on choice and thought instead of the results of our thoughts and choices.

Therefore, what is the most fundamental ethic of them all. It is one in which we have already touched on in a previous chapter. It deals with the orientation of one's own heart to either selfish or selfless means. As we talked about earlier, these can be blended into the same thing from the perspective of God and therefore our first ethic is to see as God sees. This is not only our first ethic, but also our only ethic.

I had a friend once ask me, "Do you have any extreme philosophy?" He asked this because when discussing matters of belief I continually bounced back and forth between both sides of the argument. I was as a lawyer and could answer any question with, "It depends." I said, "Yes, I do have one extreme philosophy." That philosophy is to follow God. I could think of no circumstance when following God would not be the best choice to make.

In terms of killing people, stealing, lying, I could think of moral justifications, but for disobeying God I could think of none. Therefore, my one moral rule is: to follow God.

To follow God is to walk the path he walks. It is to talk the talk he talks. It is to see what and how he sees and to be who he is. To see what he sees is to see different things. To see how he sees is to see things differently.

By seeing in a different way, you experience a different reality and become a different reality, or change who you are. Therefore, the perspective switch of which we talk about is part of this one ethical standard.

The diversity and ethics comes from the diversity of conceptions of God. Therefore, even with this foundational footing laid, we are in some aspects at the same point we were before this first rule and or law. But, in another sense we are further along in knowing that we now know that it is ethical to have an ethic.

And second, it is ethical to follow that ethic. Therefore, the process is to know that laws exist, to know what those laws are, and then to follow those laws.

Therefore, we do not prescribe any ethic except that you should know what you follow and follow what you know.

Chapter 18

The Ideal Way to Find the Ideal

We have found that people are often happier living up to the wrong ideal than not living up to the right ideal. Therefore, one component of happiness is merely doing as we suggested at the end of the last chapter, that is living what you believe.

To *be-living* what you *be-lieve* is true belief. But, is it good just to have a belief and live up to it? Or does *what* you believe have a different outcome?

If you believe the world is a certain way, everything you see will be through that lens. In fact, your mind will find proof to support what you believe. But, many of us use our minds not only to prove our beliefs to ourselves, but to prove our beliefs to others and have others' beliefs proven to us.

This is what we see through the rational debates of lawyers, theologians, and politicians. We do this with our friends, our families, and even ourselves. We try to understand the world only through the mind, we neglect one of the most powerful tools to find truth.

We discussed this tool in Chapter 13 where we discussed our epistemological approach. Finding the ideal must be a spiritual process. It must be one that starts from the heart.

Sometimes your beliefs will be rational and will be confirmed initially through the mind, but when you trust your intuition you will find the validation you think you need through a source outside the process of thinking alone.

Our intuition is guided in a universal sense. Our emotions can lead us to find the true ideal. Anger is the same for everyone. How everyone responds to the anger is based on their own personal choice. In fact, anger as the response is a personal choice in itself. With our emotions therefore, we not only respond with emotion, but also must respond to emotion.

Most of us know intuitively which emotions are positive or negative. In the negative, apathy, fear, anger, worry. In the positive, concern and curiosity, humor and creativity, love, peace, and inspiration. Everyone uses different words in different orders, but for the most part there is a consensus about which emotions are positive and which are negative.

Worry and concern might seem like the same thing, but worry is often fueled by selfish fear and concern is often for others motivated by love. Thus, one way to tell whether an emotion is positive or negative is to look at the orientation of it. And, to look at the deeper root of it.

Complete apathy is not an emotion, but is the absence of emotion. Therefore, it is death or complete darkness. It is complete inaction. Therefore, even the negative emotions have some sort of light in them and can thus be used to rise to greater light.

To move up the ladder of consciousness through an awareness of one's emotions is what can lead to finding the ideal. The ideal is positive in nature and therefore positive emotions both bring forth the ideal and are brought forth by the ideal.

A world full of love, peace, prosperity, happiness, unity, etc. is perpetuated by loving, peaceful, prosperous, happy, unifying acts. And, these acts bring forth the fruits of themselves.

To first develop awareness in yourself of your current state of consciousness (and what you are feeling) is the foundation to helping the whole world. Before you can help others or see others' needs you must be aware of what *needs* are in general. And, this awareness comes by knowing yourself first and your needs. Therefore, once you know what you need and or want, you can see these needs and or wants and others.

Seeing in others what is in you can also be applicable in determining the negative parts of your nature that need to be transformed. This here is the truth that can be applied in both the positive and the negative and is the guiding rule to find your ideal:

What you see in others that you don't like is too much in you. And, what you see in others that you do like is too little in you.

People will naturally be guided to liking positive things and positive emotions and therefore you can use your liking or disliking to guide you to positive things and positive emotions.

Transformation of self is transforming negative to positive. It can start with transforming extremely negative to less extremely negative, but the real power comes in not moving up the ladder in increments, but choosing the extreme positive immediately and always.

Happiness, love, creativity, and all things positive are always a choice. These are characteristics of people who are utilizing their divine human capacities to choose, and owning their lives.

Victims are victims only of themselves and choose to not choose. They choose to think they have no choice over the quality of their lives, and or the characteristic of their current consciousness. They let their emotions use them instead of using their emotions to serve others. They are thereby of no service to others when they are being serviced in the garage of something's wrong.

The positive focus on the positive, and look instead for what's right. They are not blind to the wrong, but choose to see right through it to the right. By seeing the right they see more of it.

They live their ideal life from moment to moment. They have no expectations or demands of others, themselves as objects, or God as an instrument to their means, but hold instead to the expectation of seeing more and more of their ideal by seeing it now.

This conscious choice to see might seem hard, but only if you see it as hard. Those who know it's easy are the ones who saw it as easy. When making the choice to see like this, anything that resists you seeing as this is the thing that need to be transformed.

Thus, by choosing the positive you see its possibility and its barriers. Barriers that would have gone unnoticed had you not chosen to see in the ideal way. And now that you see the barriers, you can more easily move them or move past them. And, you can lead others to them and through them as well.

Chapter 19

Duty of Love and Love of Duty

When it comes to doing the right things, we must also consider why we are doing them. This can be known as doing the right things for the right reason. This was a point that the philosopher Immanuel Kant, often referred to in his discourses on duty, and is a point to make here.

There are different motivations for doing the right. Fear of punishment, incentive of rewards, love, or duty. The first two are self-explanatory, but the relation between love and duty takes some extra explanation.

Duty can either be done out of love or obligation. Obligation is usually associated with one of the first two mentioned motivations. Therefore, true duty is out of love and it is redundant to speak of love and duty as separate endeavors, but instead to seek their distinction from fear and incentives by blending the two concepts. The blend comes from the idea of the duty of love and the love of duty.

First, the duty of love. Love, especially from the Christian Bible, is associated with the first two great commandments. In many religions it is emphasized likewise in such high a position. It has been said to love people not things, and use things not people. People tend to call forth a different kind of love than what we can or should give to objects.

The concept of duty can be considered even at a higher level of people. When you love the idea of duty you also love the ideas of which you are dutiful to. This love comes naturally and immediately because of the love you have for the ideator them self.

Fear of punishments and incentive of rewards is doing your duty for selfish reasons. Selfish also being the same as loving yourself. Doing your duty out of love is for unselfish reasons. It is love for the idea and concept of duty itself, the giver of the duty, and the dutiful act of which you are participating.

The love of duty itself as a concept is understanding why we are given duties. Duties are as laws, and without law could we ever be free. Truth is law and truth set you free. That which is not truth or law of the eternal and positive sense binds you.

A life without law is like a kite unbound from the earth by no string. It could never fly. However, even with the power of the law there is something above it. That is the power of the giver of the law.

Law has been ordained to serve us and occasions arise wherein one can be of greater service by breaking the law. Permission to do so will be given by the giver of the law and will be done out of love for selfless reasons. Bad men break the law for their own self gratification, while good men break the law to advance the good of all men. Knowing the difference takes much self-awareness and listening to the heart, one's intuition, or the spirit.

One must love the act of doing one's duty. *This is true happiness when you can learn to love the things you have to do.* This frictionless approach to life lets you glide through all the mundane necessities and find just as much joy in them as you do in the exciting wants of life.

Now, with the ideas established of our duty of love and our love of duty, we must examine two more components: the duty of duty and the love of love.

The duty of duty is, as we described before, the necessity of law itself. Law would have no purpose if it merely existed and was not followed. Law is one thing we can create, but should not be. Laws are eternal and therefore are not created, but discovered.

When people talk of creating new laws, they are merely refashioning them to suit a specific purpose. We have a duty to duty in that we not pollute its purpose. We must be ever careful not to make something our duty that was never intended to be so.

Now, with the love of love, it is helpful to consider what is not the love of love. That hate of love is to despise the positive connecting nature of love and the love of hate is to admire the negative disconnecting nature of hate. Love always brings together while hate always divides asunder.

The love of love is therefore then to bring together the concept of love in itself. This great uniter of everything must first be guided in every way with itself and therefore to love love is prerequisite before you can love anything else or anyone else.

Should anything be done not out of love? To do your duty without love is not doing your duty at all. Should anything be done not out of duty? To love anything or anyone that it is not your duty to love, is not a true form of love.

But, we are to love all men, even our enemies, and not love things but use them. Thus, love and duty are interwoven and reciprocal in their origin and their effect.

Chapter 20

The Sameness of the Healthy

"Happy families are all alike; every unhappy family is unhappy in its own way." — Leo Tolstoy

Inspired by Tolstoy's quote on happy families, we suggest that all healthy societies are alike in the same way and all unhealthy societies are unhealthy in their own ways. Healthy people, families, and communities are built upon the same principles. Those who failed to live up to these principles experience unhealthiness in their own terms.

How many diseases are there that plagued the body, while true health has only one standard. Sometimes someone can be unhealthy, but appear to be without disease. Yet, health is not the absence of disease. Disease is the absence of health.

The philosopher Gadamer once said, "Health is not something that is revealed through investigation but rather something that manifests itself precisely by virtue of escaping our attention."

When someone is truly healthy they are in complete unawareness of any unhealthiness in them. Being aware of a dis-comfort or a dis-ease is not the first step of acquiring an uncomfortable disease. With disease it goes in reverse from how healing operates.

With feeling, awareness is the first step. To admit one has a problem and then to make the necessary changes to heal the said problem. When one becomes aware of disease, their awareness is the last step. The changes that led to this awareness have already been undergone.

But, it is on the pivot of awareness that one can choose to either respond or ignore. This is the same for awareness of social ills in our society.

That which we are not aware of is not a problem for us and therefore how could we go about solving. A truly healthy society would be no awareness of any unhealthiness by anyone in society. If there is one person in society with awareness of unfairness or social decay, the whole society is not whole, though many might think it so.

This calls for a universal consciousness. The way that we can all connect to be conscious of all. Universal consciousness is both a metaphysical terminology, but through technology can also is becoming a physical reality.

We are in a better place today than ever before to be connected with all parts of ourselves as a society. Society has grown more conscious with this better awareness. However, with this better awareness we are given the opportunity to respond or the chance to ignore.

How does one go about responding to the needs of society?

In the body, there is both a collaborative effort among the whole body, but also specific jobs that specific parts perform to help bring balance and restoration to the parts in need. All cannot be white blood cells in society, because we need the constant nourishment transmitted through red blood cells to stay alive for the white blood cells to do their part.

Therefore, we are interdependent and inter-independent with all. Ancient peoples and many modern people today believe and see the value in eating organs. They carry the philosophy that to best help the liver one must eat liver. The ancients had healthier organs, because they didn't exclude organs from their diets. They ate all of the animal.

For this reason, liver is the best food for the liver. Bones for the bones, brain for the brain, heart for the heart. This might sound pretty grotesque in Western society, and though I am not prescribing it completely as part of the recipe for a transformed society, the principles are relevant to our discussion here.

The social ill one takes up in their response to help cure is the one that they are most aware of and in a position to respond. They are response-able or responsible for this part of the whole society. As they help this, it becomes irrelevant for them and a new problem will surface to which they can respond to again. This continual process will continue until no response is needed, because no stimulus is given.

In this state, the stimuli that call our response are the ones that lead to more and more of the same. The principles of health. What are the principles of a healthy society? The ones that all healthy societies share? They are both listed throughout the book and will be touched on in the next chapter. They include both principles of human rights and duties and social rights and duties.

Chapter 21

Principles of a Healthy Society

We will try to keep our discussion on the principles of a healthy society and individual as basic as possible. Which makes sense, in that we are talking of principles. Which, if complex would probably not be basic at all. Therefore, the simplicity of our principles is their validation as well. We will look at an individual and examine them as both integrated beings and the diversified parts of being they include.

The three parts of man that must be healthy for the entire man to be healthy are a healthy body, a healthy mind, and a healthy spirit. And, a healthy balance between the three. And, the proper ordering of the three.

The ordering is spirit, then mind, then body. The balance is balanced. All equal. People who are too caught up in one and neglect the other parts of them are imbalanced. People are imbalanced in all if they are imbalanced in one. An imbalanced mind hurts the spirit and vice versa and also including the body.

But, they cannot just all be in balance with each other, but must also be balanced in themselves. As well, they must not only be in complete balance within themselves as a whole person, but also must be in balance with others in their society. They cannot be balanced with someone who is in imbalance. Their imbalance can cause an imbalance in them.

It is actually part of your own balancing to help balance others. And, others balancing to help you balance. And thus all balance all. Therefore, one of the best ways to overcome a given weakness is to help someone else overcome that same weakness.

Now, because balancing includes things spiritual, this balancing is something that cannot be observed empirically in its entirety. This balance is not something one must consciously always keep on their mind, because that would be an imbalance of the mind.

Just as does everything, balancing starts with the spirit. The reason for hope is that the spirit has an already inherent balancing disposition within it to balance you with you and you with your neighbor. Therefore, as you respond to the feelings of imbalance which are promptings to change, you will change and balance in this.

Therefore, one of the most chief characteristics of a healthy society is responding to the spirit within them and to the spirits without. Disease is literally dis-ease or imbalance. A spiritual disease can manifest itself in the physical form through a disease of the body. When a body disease is truly cured it will be cured at the spiritual level. The healthy society knows this and practices it.

If someone is overweight, it is not enough just to stop eating as much. One has to ask why did they start eating so much in the first place. We often use our bodies to console our souls and when we abuse our bodies we abuse our already abused souls. A healthy soul would not harm its own body or any other body's bodies or souls.

Therefore, we have a duty not to harm others or ourselves. We keep this duty by keeping it first on the spiritual level. Emotions help you to see into these connections between the mind, body, and spirit. Emotions can weigh you down spiritually, cause your mind to race relentlessly, and even stimulate a physiological response.

A healthy society is emotionally mature. They know how to both handle their own emotions and respond to the emotions of others. In their responses, they do not react, but create through a complete integrated mind, body, and spirit approach, a creative response to the agitator.

If someone blows up at them in a rage of anger, they can be as calm as an un-raging river. They merely allow the other's emotions to roll over and pass them like stones in a river. The faster and harder the river flows over them, the more smooth they themselves become. But, if they try to resist they can find themselves being washed downstream with the other or becoming a dam to the other's progression and their own as well.

A truly spirit led mind and body will lead the mind and body to perfect balance. The spirit originates from perfect balance and therefore exists naturally in this state. We imbalance it through over-exertions of the mind and body, suppressing it. But, when we allow it by submitting our other parts of ourselves, it gives more power to the whole being than the other parts could ever imagine to contain.

We can only work so hard before we get tired. We can only think for so long before our brains are fried. But, the spirit is self generating in that the more it is utilized the more fired up it becomes. Yet, knowing its perfect place, it knows the limitations of the mortal mind and body and therefore gives its due regards to the proper functioning and maintenance of the three.

It is the mediator between what we think and do. It can guide our thoughts and our actions. It helps by telling us if what we say is congruent with how we act. It can tell us if there is an imbalance in this aspect as well as an imbalance with all the aspects.

When the spirit is suppressed, it is sometimes necessary to be liberated by a spirit outside of it. Its main orientation is to self-reliance. Therefore, more important than learning to obey a spirit with-out, is learning to obey the spirit with-in.

The spirit within is the center of our choice. It is the center of learning and growth. It is the center of the individual and the center of society. It is the central principle upon which all societies that are healthy share in common.

There is not any society that is not healthy that is not *not* unhealthy first and foremost spiritually. The one unhealthiness of spirit can manifest itself in a variety of social ills, but the one pill for this ill is to pay the bill via a spiritual fill. When people and society are filled with the spirit, it alone leads to the fulfillment of every other part that makes all the other parts full and filled in themselves.

Chapter 22

Social Self-Control

Most of the time when we think of social control, we are thinking of structural conditions in which we ourselves are controlled in society. However, there is a different type of social control of which we will speak here. This type of social control is that which is more similar to the self-control of an individual. It is a self-control of the social by the social.

Structural control is both forced upon us by the external world and enforced by the external world. Social self-control is voluntarily taken upon oneself, speaking collectively, the external suggestions of a society. The suggestions are merely this. They are not enforced formally, but their enforcement is no less as powerful as if they were.

Think about St. Patrick's Day in America. No one is forced to wear green, but if they don't they are liable to be pinched. The pinching is a form of social self-control. This might be part of the culture specific to St. Patrick's Day, but the principle is universal in its scope. The principle is that by not conforming to a socially prescribed and socially accepted principle, one must receive some sort of social sanction.

This is the idea of social norms. These are not laws, which are external and structural, but unwritten expectations held by the majority of the population. If it is not the majority that holds these beliefs, then it is not normal and therefore not a norm.

Norms are a way that a society self-regulates or controls itself. They are also the way that a society ultimately frees itself from itself.

When it is the norm to keep the law, the law no longer needs to exist. True laws are unchanging and thus should never be manipulated to adhere to ever-changing social norms. In our modern world, the law has been up for election, and the vote usually swings in the favor of the norms, disregarding corruption and financial lobbying.

But, even with the constraining structural component of the law, the more important way to transform a society is to be aware and actively engaged in the following and forming of righteous norms. Righteous not meaning anything religious, but ethical. Norms that are right.

When what is right is the norm, that which is wrong will be sanctioned by the society through societal self-control. Wrongness will not need a special task force to deal with it, because the people at large will enforce their own sanctions. There will be as many policemen as there men to police. This societal internal control is what allows for the true control of societal external control.

When and where is control's proper time and place?

True control would control the process through which the process of control is controlled. The process of control we adhere to now is one of top to bottom. Through a democratic approach, the bottom has a voice to the top and therefore in some sense control controls them.

Government is where this occurs on a collective consensus, and religion is where this occurs through an individual's senses. In the collective, consensus is sought. On individual level, one seeks to make sense of one's own life and control it accordingly.

It is interesting to note that both politics and religion are two topics that are most often shunned by our society in casual conversation. Almost as a form of social self-control. Yes we have the structural freedom of speech and of religion, but the norms say it is wrong or at least dangerous to talk too much about your own beliefs regarding government and or religion.

With this fear, comes the foreshadowing of structural adoption of protection. Instead of being protected to be able to have one's own beliefs, we will be protected from others' beliefs. This would be the structural control of these two fundamental forms of social control.

These two forms are most fundamental because *religion is how we choose to govern ourselves and government is who we choose to let govern us*. Religion is between the individual and God. Government is between the individual and society. In a true religion, the top is not voted in by the people, but put in by the God. In a true government, the top is not voted in by the people, but put in by the Society.

You might ask, "What's the difference between the people and the society?" The people are the actual people, but the society is what the people actually believe. Therefore, if the politicians are corrupt, it is because the people are corrupt. But, on the flipside, if they are uncorrupt or righteous, they were put in by a righteous people.

The vote doesn't matter as much as the voters. The candidates themselves are part of the voting pool in that they can vote for themselves. The quality of the candidates and their supporters is what dictates the outcome.

If they are corrupt and people are corrupt they will win.

If they are corrupt and people are not corrupt they will lose.

If they are not corrupt and people are corrupt they will lose.

And, if they are not corrupt and people are not corrupt they will win.

Corruptness is a societal additive and attitude. It is the norms of society. The voice of the people do not only choose who to represent them, but what they represent by who they choose. Therefore, it is more the ideologies that exist among the people than the latest opinion poll of the people.

As a society, we therefore self-control ourselves through the political process and the related legal system. Though, once in these forms they become structural and not social.

For social transformation to occur, the transformation of the social by the social must start at the social level. The social level is what feeds into structural and a personal level is what feeds into the social level.

Therefore, the transformation of the social level by the personal level must start at the personal level. And, the social nature of personal beings is what feeds into the personal level. And, the structural level of the social self is what determines one's social nature. Let's look at this in more detail.

Chapter 23

The Structural Level of the Social Self of the Individual

When we say it all starts at the personal level when it comes to social transformation, we mean what we say. But, the personal level has different levels within itself.

------Personal Transformation-------

<u>Internal and Individual</u>

Personal self

Social self

Structural self

-------Social Transformation------

<u>External and Collective</u>

Personal society

Social society

Structural society

The structural level of the social self of the individual is the level of being. The social self level is the level of doing. The personal self level is the level of knowing or thinking. These categories are available to the external and collective types. We can be aware of our own thoughts and sometimes even assume we "know what the other person is thinking."

Obviously, when it comes to the social, we can only assume without asking and then we can only assume the answer they give is true. It is the same for us. We even say sometimes, "I don't know what I was thinking." We ourselves have thoughts that are not our own. Where do these thoughts come from? They come from the social and structural parts of us.

The social comes from interaction. As we said, it is the doing level of the self. Therefore, doing is synonymous with action. Interaction literally means action between (*inter*). The social self within us is when we dialogue between two different parts of us. This is how we make decisions internally and this process translates to the external world. This interaction is what mediates the structural external part of our internal being and the personal internal part of our internal being.

The structural part of our internal being is who we are when no one is looking. This is what we call integrity. Who we are implies that our beingness is fixed and real. It is not a presentation of self, but is both the cause and effect of the other parts of the self. During a dialogue within ourselves we come to conclusions and adopt certain theories to be true. We let these theories constitute who we are and thus they are what we play out throughout all levels.

True personal transformation is a structural change of the innermost part of the self. True social transformation is a structural change of outermost part of society. A perfect person or someone who is perfect cannot do anything imperfect or think anything imperfect (Remember when we say cannot we refer more specifically to will not, because technically they could, due to the inherent freedom to choose). Likewise, with a perfect society nothing imperfect would ever be done or ever be thought of by the members of it, both as individuals in it and collectives of it.

Just as all life springs up around a spring, the spring's existence as a spring is dependent upon by water running off into it. This is the same for people and society. All social life springs from the personal level of human existence, but it is through the external existence of humans that trickles down into the humans making them what they are.

Without symbols, or words, how could we ever even have a conversation within our own heads, decide what to do or who to be? Therefore, the relation between man and society is concomitant. However, just as it is multidirectional, it is also multiplicital in the different ways each way affects the other way.

What came first, society or the man? Or better yet, men or man? And, though our gender biased language uses the word men, the plural form of this can include women or a woman. Maybe the age-old question, "What came first the chicken or the egg?" should be rephrased as "What came first, the chicken*s* or the egg?" It takes two to make an egg. And, it takes only one egg to make a chicken. But, the fact that we still have chickens must mean it must have taken two eggs as well. Therefore, even further, "What came first, the chickens or the eggs?"

If this is the question, then our original question could be rephrased as what came first "Man and Women or Men and Women?"

Truly, the best answer we can give to this is both. In the chicken analogy, it is chickens with eggs in them and eggs with chickens in them. The chickens have eggs in them in a capacity or pre-embryonic potential necessarily constituted by having more than one chicken of two different sexes.

The same as with the eggs. The eggs needed two of these chickens of two different sexes both with the capacities of the characteristics of the chickens before mentioned.

Therefore, it is an infinite loop and is why we find the question so amusing. But, with infinity we know something of its origin. Infinity can only come from infinity. Eternity from eternity and spirituality from spirituality. Thus in these endless loops we must seek the end by seeking the maker of the loop.

Most people think of this as God. God created both the chicken and the egg or the chicken and egg and the egg in the chicken at the same time. He, being infinite, created infinite beings. He created the man and men or the personal and the social at the same time.

Even in the Christian story of Adam and Eve, Adam is created first and then Eve, but Adam only becomes capable of becoming one flesh or full and complete once and only after Eve's creation has been completed. The breathing out of life into man was the word or the symbols which make man possible. Therefore, also, "In the beginning was the word, and the word was with God, and the word was God"(John 1:1). To make vocal external noise, we inevitably breathe out. Therein, is the breath of life. The words, the symbols we use to dialogue between ourselves in our self and between ourselves with each other.

Thoughts are but internal words, and speaking is but external thoughts. Thinking and speaking are what create the man personally and create men or society.

The world can never be any better structurally without the betterment of both internal and external structures.

Chapter 24

Against Againstness and For Forness

This is a theoretical orientation that will be helpful to share here, but will be more helpful if applied to every situation in your own life and or any social organization of which you are part. This orientation is to be for the positive instead of being against the negative.

In so many social change efforts we often hear, "eradicate poverty, the coalition against homelessness, mothers against drunk driving, stop the one percent, etc." though we do hope to put an end to these things, when negativity is our end, it will never have an end.

It is like a basketball player shooting free-throws saying to them self, "don't miss, don't miss, don't miss." They will work themselves up into such mental confusion that the reason they missed is because they messed up in their mind first which translated into their actual missing in reality.

When you say the negative, the negative always remains. If health manifests itself as it escapes our attention as Gadamer said, then by continually putting emphasis on the negative our attention will continually be on the negative, or the unhealthy, and we will continually find more and more of the negative.

This might sound similar to the law of attraction. For example, if you hate a cause that someone represents and you verbally or nonverbally persecute the others for their belief in their cause, you will do more to reinforce their own point of view than relieve them of it. *Through your intolerance, you attract more things to be intolerant of.* The greatest irony is those who are intolerant of intolerance.

To really relieve someone of a wrong point of view, you must relieve yourself of the negative emotions attached to that wrong point of view. Though what we'll say next, might make you disregard everything we've said up to now, you might find that by changing yourself from a negative to a positive orientation might also change your view of the other.

By changing *you,* you change your view. By changing your view they are more likely to change their view. This is the only way to come to unity.

Thus, by not being against the negative parts of their view but for the positive parts of their view, the positive will grow. You will attract more things to be positive of and they might even come from the people who you used to hate.

This happens on an individual level, but also socially. It is the sad phenomenon of groupthink that leads masses of people to hate masses of people. It only takes one in the group to stand up to the group to help them to rethink themselves. The one person who stands up must trust that positivity has infinitely more power to it than the negative.

When they stand up, they do not stand alone because everything everyone stands for is for them. Even when people think they are against you, they are in reality against themselves by being against anything. By being for all you are a being-for-all. Meaning, you exist to help, to serve, and to teach.

Againstness is selfish. Forness is selfless. *Everything negative is fueled by selfishness and everything positive fuels selflessness.* The negative is acted upon by the negative within your heart while the positive acts upon that which is outside of your heart in positive ways.

Forness is different than non-againstness and againstness is different than non-forness. To not be for or against something is to be neutral. Neutrality is a helpful place to come from, but to best help the place you're in and want to go, you must choose a side. In choosing a side, you can stay neutral by choosing both sides. You choose the positive from both. Therefore, you are still neutral, but all at the same time.

With this perspective, you are fighting for an ideology and not for a sociology. You are able to separate the people from their ideas. You are not against anyone, but you are not not against anything. There are things, or more correctly, ideas that you are against. But, what you are most against is againstness, but instead of being against againstness and thus being against yourself, you choose to be for forness and for yourself and all other things, or ideas, that you yourself believe to be positive and true.

This is the separation of the sin and the sinner. If you look at people as sinners they will stay as such and become more true to how you see them. When you look at them as the righteousness they are, you allow them to become that which they have within them. People will become how they are seen and especially if they are sinners. If they are righteous, they are independent and free enough to choose who they want to become, but if they are sinners as you suppose, then they need your support to see them not as who they really are not.

Though they might have sins or weaknesses, who doesn't? Only one doesn't, and that is the being like whom you are trying to be, a fully-transformed being. A being focused on potential opportunity and not potential risk. The risk of life has already been taken, therefore by seeing the risk in negative terms we will only self fulfill the negative portions of that risk. But, when we see the positive, we see the potential in the risk no longer becomes conscious to us. As it is no longer conscious to us, it no longer has power over us.

This is the same lesson. Those who see sin only know it because it is in them. If you yourself think yourself to be in the right, then act in the right by being *for* the right, and by being for what's right and everyone and everything. You can never go wrong by doing, seeing, or being in the right.

Chapter 25

What Would You Do if There Were No World to Change?

That which you would do if the world was to already be changed, is that which you must do if the world is to readily be changed.

What will we do after true social transformation? If transforming yourself and others is the most important and urgent thing to do, what would we do if and when we accomplish what we are seeking to do? If we cannot transform ourselves, or transform others, then what will occupy our time and our attention?

From an eternal perspective there can be a variety of answers. But, for the most part we do not know exactly what we will do. Though, we can assume that we will be participating in the activities of the realm of the transformed. And, we know that in part the realm of the transformed continues to help the realms of the untransformed. In some aspect, we too will probably participate in this continual transformation process.

However, once we are perfect we cannot become any more perfect and therefore our progression is not in terms of becoming more perfect in selfhood, but perfecting more selves in Godhood. We will be as God is, for God was as we are. Or, we will be as transformed as the transformed, just as the transformed were once untransformed as us. This is eternity.

But, in a more temporal sense, there are implications that implicate us toward action now in the present. That is, what do you do when nothing needs doing?

We make the assumption that transformation and existence altogether needs to happen and continue, but beyond these assumptions where does our orientation to action reside?

This is really the distinction between need and want. We only still exist because we want to exist. Therefore, it is because of this want that we need to do certain things. Want is always the vision and need is always the conditions for that vision. When you need water, it is because you want to live. Therefore, want is truly the root of need.

Many times we think want goes after need. We think after we satisfy our basic needs, we can then give attention to satisfying our greatest wants. But, it is what we label as our greatest needs that are our greatest wants. We want to live, but why?

We want to change the world, but why? After all the trouble we go through from trying to change the world, what is it for? If we learn to enjoy the journey of changing so much, then we will feel empty at the end. That is, unless we also fill ourselves now with what we will do then. It is only by doing this that emptiness can be prevented and non-emptiness can be secured. It is truly doing this that is part of a true transformation.

Many times people think linearly, especially when in college, that they want to do some sort of work that would earn them a lot of money so that they could then go and help a lot of people. This type of thinking however, is conditional. It is a, "if I earn a lot of money, then I will help a lot of people." The amount of people being helped is dependent upon the amount of money being made. What does this imply?

This implies that one is not helping people by earning money, but only by giving money. Therefore, is this post career giving back only a reparation for all the getting you had to do through the first part of your life? Are you merely trying to fix what you broke? Here is a new perspective.

What if you could serve people in the same way that you want to after your career in your career now? If you want to be a teacher, then you can be a teacher now. If you want to be a certain teacher in a certain place then start teaching in the certain way that would make certain your placement into the certain teaching position.

This is not anything new, but is a reminder. You can do whatever you want to do in whatever you are doing now. It is just as much loving what you do as it is doing what you love. Therefore, the question is not what do you love to do, but what is right to do?

This question of rightness is at the core of our first question. What to do after all is done.

The most simple answer to this is to do that which is right. But, what is right? Obviously, when there are people in need, then what is right would be to help them get what they need. But, as we discovered, needs come from wants and therefore you can always help people get what they want.

Will there ever be an end of wanting? No. Want is limitless, infinite, unquenchable. It is both what leads to our greatest joy and our greatest sorrow. It is the duality of the results it yields that allows the results to be yielded.

Since wanting can never be satiated, neither can not wanting. We think of apathy as not wanting to do anything, when in reality it is just wanting to do nothing. The want to do nothing is not evil in itself, but only if it is for itself.

We can do nothing or want to do nothing as a result of not wanting to do anything- in a positive light. This desire for inaction is supreme contentment. This sort of contentment should be as fixed and unchanging as is the nature of desire itself. Though, with this contentment and its desire for nothing comes its opposite desire for everything. You can call this discontent, in reality just as beautiful as is being content.

Obviously, we are not content with the way the world is, but never should we be. As beings of wanting we will always want more.

And therefore, after all we want to do is done, we will still want to *do* after all. What to do is not as important as want to do. It is the want that will tell them what. And, until we get to that point, there is no point in trying to pinpoint what we will do then. For, what we know now is what we want now. And, what we will want then is dependent on what we will know then. But, though that nonetheless does not leave us without a want to know what we will want then, we can know now what we want most now, and do it now. Both loving the activity of transforming and loving the activities we transform for.

Chapter 26

Personal and Social Processes of Teaching and Learning

It has been said, "Give a man a fish, feed him for a day. Teach a man to fish, feed him for a lifetime." But, as we mentioned before, we want to add at least one more level to this proposition. "Teach a man to teach men how to fish, feed the man's community for a lifetime." "Teach a man to teach men how to teach men how to fish, feed the world."

You could go on and on with this teaching. The idea is that we take it further than just helping others and helping others to help themselves. We help others to help others help others to help others.

There are really an infinite amount of levels, but we will mention five. In the first, you give a man a fish or help him.

In the second, you teach a man to fish or help him to help himself.

In the third, the man who now knows how to fish has enough to give to others. Or, you help him to help others.

In the fourth, you teach the man how to teach men how to fish and therefore you help him to help others help themselves.

In the fifth, you teach a man how to teach men how to give, therefore you help him to help others help others.

Now, this is not just for fishing. It applies to everything. Learning, and applying what we learn are the two cyclical operations that lead to personal and social progress. If you could learn perfectly and execute what you learned perfectly then you would be in a sense perfect. Therefore, we must learn how to learn and learn how to apply what we learn.

On the opposite side of the spectrum, we must teach how to teach and teach how to inspire others to action. Action is the end goal of all teaching, because knowledge without application is of no worth. It remains as a dollar bill to an indigenous tribe. If it has no context in the real world, or social world, then it is of no real use or social value.

Service is the application stage of the learning process. Learning in its complete sense entails application and therefore maybe no distinction between the two is necessary. When you truly learn, you truly apply. Non-applying is not true learning. Therefore, the teacher's role is to teach knowledge, but if this knowledge is transferred into action then the teaching was not complete. Therefore, true teachers teach more than information, but teach transformation. For it has been said by Elbert Hubbard, "No written word nor spoken plea can teach young minds what they should be, not all the books on all the shelves but what the teachers are themselves."

Learning and applying is essentially the process of change. Through education, true education which implies action, we change ourselves and others. It is not a change that happens only in the mind in that you used to know 100 facts and now you know 120. But, it is a change of both the mind and the heart. This change in both the mind and the heart leads the body to perform the actions of change into the external world. This is a change of being. As being changes, so do the behaviors of the being.

Therefore, both social and personal transformations are dependent upon the learning process. And, learning is dependent upon some sort of teaching. Now, there can be self-teaching which is therefore self-learning, but in terms of intervention it sometimes takes a teacher to inspire self-teaching.

Self-teaching is what true teaching really is. There really is no way to transfer knowledge from one head to another. We are not like USB drives in that through connecting we can streamline what is in our heads into the heads of others, but work more like Wi-Fi. We help others to connect to the greater source of knowledge that we ourselves are connected to. Then, we lead them through a process of diving into the source of knowledge. We help them to navigate, but do not navigate for them. Or, should we say, we *need* not navigate for them, or *should not* navigate for them either.

In the beginning of learning, a directive approach might be more necessary to help them out, but as they learn they will learn to learn for themselves and this is prerequisite for them being able to help others to learn period and also for others to learn for themselves. This is related to the concept of dependency and independency.

You want your students to be independent and be able to teach themselves or learn for themselves, but what about the higher ideals of interdependence and inter-independence. How do these apply to learning and teaching?

Remember that interdependence and inter-independence our social phenomena. They take more than two. More than one teacher and more than one learner. It is an organization of people and circumstance wherein all are learning from all. This is when people get together and engage in a collaborative learning process. They both learn from the source, but also learn from each other. "For where two or three are gathered together in my name, there am I in the midst of them" (Matthew 18:20).

They are gathered in the name of learning, learning how to live up to the name of the learned. And, as they are together they come together to know what means what for who. This immediately allows them to have a shared meaning that each of them could not have gained on their own through their own self-learning processes.

For true social transformation to take place, this type of learning must also take place. There must be a way for the whole of society to learn in the same way. Until we can do this, we will all know the same things in the same way, but think others think of the same things in different ways.

This is part of a dialectical process of ideas. But, this process does not just stay in the mind, but is carried out through action. Therefore, there is a material dialectic as well as each person connects with the real world through their actions and the effects of these actions.

Chapter 27

Trust In and Work Towards Salvation

There is a quote, often used in religious contexts, by Thomas Aquinas that says, "Work as if everything depends on you and pray as though everything depends on God." This quote was specifically addressed to individuals, but can apply socially as well.

There are many Christians who faithfully look forward to the fulfillment of the prophecy of the second coming of Christ. Yet, I would argue that this one-way "faithful" anticipation is really not true faith at all.

True faith implies action. Just like we must work like it all depends on us to receive God's help in our personal lives, it is the same for social transformation. Therefore, even Christians need to engage in the work of transforming the world because it is part of the necessary ingredient to be able to pray with true faith and bring about the actual transformation they yearn for. They cannot just wait passively for the world to be transformed for them. Those who do have no part in this transformed world.

We have tried to keep our argument simple and our philosophies concise, but when all is said and done the greatest simplicity is to trust in victory over the complexities of such a task as ours.

There are so many variables still to be figured out, but it is in the simple suggestions prescribed that these next variables will even appear. We will move from grace to grace, line upon line, precept upon precept in our individual transformations and as a society and its transformation.

Throughout, complete collective physical engagement in the actual process of transformation will be necessary, but so will complete collective mental and spiritual engagement be too. The mental exertion will be that of maintaining a vision through the fog. The spiritual aspiration will be that of trusting and taking steps forward in the fog. So often we pray for clarity when we really just need to pray for faith. Having a vision and faithfully stepping forward towards it takes trust.

All of the other ways of social transformation are based on well-researched plans and methods that supposedly guarantee success while though unguaranteed-ably they often cause more harm than help. It is only through transformation in the way and the order we prescribe that can only lead to help and not harm. Unless, of course, the transformation is undergone in a direction contrary to the light and truth.

The negative transformation would be something as intentional as the positive transformation. Yet, in modern progress all is said to be done in the intention of positive progress, while many latent dysfunctions unintentionally yield negative progress. This might be what C. S. Lewis referred to when he said, "The world of business has done so much that never needed doing."

It has been said that the smallest deed is worth more than the greatest intention. It is therefore the actual amount of transformation that takes place in the people themselves that is counted more than any external technological progress our society and culture could ever create. For, transformation is the only true measure of our deeds.

These creations of technologies are really done out of a lack of trust and an unwillingness to work. The modern-day consumer seeks convenience and security. That which will make their lives easier or less frightening is worth purchasing.

Transformation can be easy, but the natural resistance to it is what makes it hard. It can seem frightening, but it is always a step to a place of truer security. That is the irony of the illusion of progress. That which seems to help often doesn't and that which appears to *not* often does.

Why does transformation take trust and work? And, what type of trust and work is it really?

The type of trust it is, is the type of trust it takes to work in a trusting way that can give you a process that you can trust to give you the outcomes you desire. It is the type of trust it takes to ride a bike without training wheels for the first time. In doing so, you transform your way of transporting yourself.

It is the type of trust that it takes to know that after you assembled an object or a machine, it will function properly. Any carelessness in the assembly will inevitably fill your mind with doubt. Therefore, maybe it is not the actual mistake of assembly that causes dysfunction, but the lack of trust in the assembly due to the dysfunctional carelessness that causes dysfunction.

Carelessness and doubt become dysfunctions in themselves. Never caring or never believing is at the bottom of the pit of negativity. This resulting apathy results in results to be apathetic of. It is caring and believing that secure the security of which you care for and can believe in.

It is trustfully working and working trustfully that works every time, forming a process you can trust.

In terms of social transformation, the process is personal transformation. When you trust that the inevitable fruit of collective personal transformations is that of social transformation, then you will work with this intention and the trusting hope of its fruition incomplete social transformation. When you work towards it, you will begin to trust it more because you will see the fruits and evidence before they are physically manifest.

Therefore, it is only those who trust initially who can trust completely. Those who don't believe will only confirm their unbelief through their unbelief. Those who do believe will see what they believe and thus be affirmed in their beliefs. Therefore, the greater question than Shakespeare proposed might be "to believe or not to believe."

You might ask, "believe what?" We would say, "believe in the power of believing." Trust in trust. Trust in work. Work in trust. And, work in work. By having the complete integration of these concepts within themselves and with each other, within ourselves and with each other we will see the fruits of our beliefs. We will see the social transformation for which we so urgently seek.

We trust that it will come, but our trust alone cannot make it come. Therefore, we trust that all will come to trust that it will come. As we trust it, we will work towards it. And, as we work towards it, our trust in it will grow ever more.

Chapter 28

Stop Trying to Change the World

You often find what you seek at the precise moment you stop looking for it. This is the paradox of positive fulfillment. It has been said of happiness, relationships, and success. It might sound too good to be true or at least too easy. What do we mean by not looking?

Reaching the level of not looking comes only after persistent seeking. It is the seeking that qualifies you to receive. But, true reception is a gift and therefore is not to be found by merits of your seeking. Therefore, you must cease to seek in order for what you seek to come to you.

In our ambitious world, we pursue what we want. But, one must keep the mindset and faith that what they want is also pursuing them. When you believe this, you no longer need to frantically seek it. You are seeking it in a different way.

One approach to this is to seek and wear yourself out to the point of not wanting to seek anymore. At this moment, that which you want will be yours. The devolved approach would be to believe in this and give up your search with the attitude of passive patience. That evolved approach is to believe in this and give yourself up to the search with an attitude of active patience.

There is a difference between giving up the search and giving yourself up to the search or giving up yourself, however you wish to look at it. When you give yourself up to the search you put yourself in the hands of the great searcher or great searching power of the universe. The great searcher will search for you and drive you to it while drive it to you, without you having to drive yourself crazy searching for it. It will search for you and you will search for it, but your searching for it will be unlike its searching for you.

Its searching for you is always and has always been happening. It could find you anytime and anywhere. In fact, its location is always closer than you think both geographically and chronologically. It could happen as soon as now and as close as here. It is by moving yourself away from the here and now that you look everywhere else but here and now.

I remember my grandma one time looking everywhere for her pencil. She came to me and asked me if I had seen it. I looked at her and saw it literally on her. She had tucked it between her ear and her hair.

These are always funny stories and circumstances, but so is every story of success in finding what you've always been looking for. How it is in front of you, but that you don't see it is one of the greatest realizations. Realization in a conscious sense, but also realization as a level of consciousness.

The level of a being fully realized is the highest level of consciousness. It is what transformation is all about. It is reaching this state that all other states of affairs that you are reaching for will reach for you. By being in harmony with this, all will harmoniously come to abide with you.

It is therefore not seeking what you want, but seeing what you want and everything that is always present before you. You therefore start to see what you want and thus it is already yours. By seeing it, you find it, and you didn't have to seek it because you were always seeing it.

It's always more about waking up to your life then, than it is about taking your life up a notch. Your life as it is meant to be is already at its highest state of being. You merely need to wake up to it to see it. Infinite potential and opportunity are always here. With this in mind, there is no need for regret or resentment because all can be healed through waking up to this possibility.

Now, what are the things that keep you asleep. You are asleep by not living true to who you are, which is ironic because living true to who we are is both a result and the cause of waking up. You wake up and choose who you are all at the same time. Though, when you wake up to the fact that it is always a choice that you can always choose to wake up whenever you want. Thus, being more intentional you can live more intentionally.

Theoretically, if we said we wanted to make X amount of money today, we could do it. Napoleon Hill is famous for saying, "Whatever the mind can conceive and believe, it can achieve." Therefore, the only limits are the limits you place on the place and time for things to come and all non-achieving is merely a lack of belief and desire. Sometimes the external world can influence this lacking, but the personal agent never lacks enough belief and desire within them to overcome it.

Therefore, it is wiser to seek to see all things than to seek to find one thing. When you are open to the infinite possibility, you allow something even greater than you could ever seek for to come. When you seek for one thing you limit what you are looking for to one thing. This limit is opposite of the limitless reality which is available to you. And thus, you often don't find what you seek until you change what you seek to find. By not seeking you find, but by not finding any one thing you also seek and find everything you could ever want.

For example, let's say you were looking for a boyfriend or girlfriend. In seeking wisely, you would give yourself to a date, but not to a certain name or individual. Thus, respecting the choice of others, but not dis-respecting the power of your own choice. You find what you seek by focusing more on what you want and less on how you want it to come.

It is the world we live in that seeks to live in a world they think they don't live in currently, when in reality there is nothing more to the world than the world itself. It is the world in itself or the world within the world that is the only possibility to change. It is this world that is here now and it is this world that we can create, not by trying but by being created. Which, our mere existence alone attests to our beingness already have been beinged.

Chapter 29

Accepting the World as Changed

What is the difference between accepting the world to change and expecting the world to change? Accepting the world to change is accepting it toward change. Expecting the world to change is excepting it to any effort you make to change it.

To change the world, we must accept it as it is. True acceptance is expecting nothing. Yet, expecting need not be evil in itself. It is expecting everything to happen while accepting full heartedly whatever happens. One is an expectation of demand, while the other is an expectation of preference.

If we demand the world to change, it will only change contrary to our demands. But, if we prefer it to change a certain way, and accept it with love for it as the way it is, this love will be reciprocated and the world will seek to give us what we want. It will want to please us by giving us what we prefer. It will change as a result of our accepting it the way it is.

Therefore, we can expect based on hope and preference while still accepting it based on what we see *in* it, not what we see *for* it.

By accepting it, you help it to see for it self. It is only by it seeing for itself that it can ever accomplish the vision it was intended to accomplish. Just as people individually have a purpose, so do we as collectivities. The world has a purpose, and so does the earth.

No one can expect anyone to do anything that they themselves do not expect for themselves. This demanding form of expectation meets itself with failed expectations when others do not meet themselves up to the expectations of others.

By expecting nothing, you are pleased with anything. By expecting everything, you are displeased with anything less than everything. By accepting everything, you are pleased with anything. By accepting nothing you are displeased with everything.

It is therefore necessary to not think of changing the world in terms of, "I'm going to change you because you need it." But, "I want you/love you and that's never going to change." The one is a demand placed on the other, while the other is a preference for the other.

One's relationship to the other is conditional upon them changing, while the other relationship is unconditional or unchanging. This relationship says, "I will love you no matter what." The other says, "I will love you only if."

If we are to change the world, we cannot use ifs. Therefore, when we are to change the world we should only use whens. Whens are both faithful and more accurate. It is not *if* the world change, but *when* the world changes. Because, the world is always changing, and *if* is untrue, and the *when* is merely a reflection of what's really happening. Your preferences come into play in the deciding of how the actual change will play out.

If it is to be a change in the positive direction, then only positive orientations of mind toward the change can yield it. Accepting is positive, but expecting is negative. However, what is the negative form of accepting?

The negative form of accepting is one void of love. It is apathy or non-caring. It says, "I don't care what you do because I don't care for you." While, the positive form of acceptance says, "I don't care what you do because I will always care for you."

Acceptance always is acceptance of something. Accepting in the positive is an acceptance of the beingness of the other even if the other doesn't accept themselves. It is by accepting them for who they are that they will be who they truly are and thus be truly changed.

What does the world expect from us? Nothing. That is speaking of the world in the true sense of what it really is. But, it can equally be said that it expects everything. It is the same for it as it is for us. It demands nothing us, but prefers everything for us. Because it prefers everything for us, we do not need to prefer anything for ourselves, but give all our preference to the world. It will accept our gifts to it if we accept it and its gifts to us.

It best takes on the form of gratitude when we accept and expect in the positive sense of both words. And, it takes a form of ingratitude if we accept or expect in the negative sense of both words. Thus, gratitude for the world as it is and as it could be is accepting and expecting. Tied with gratitude is faith. Faith to receive and faith to give.

It is not the type of faith that looks past the bad to the good, but one that looks to the good and the bad passes away. By looking past the bad you notice it, and thus it takes note of it being noticed. The good never takes note of it being noticed, because it is so preoccupied with noticing the good in others. By only seeing the good, it is easy to accept it. Therefore, the faith is a way to see and be and not a way to think or do.

When we see what can be, or what truly is, then what is can truly be what it is. And, to be the change you wish to see in the world is to see the change you yourself wish to be in the world as already here.

It is this perspective that will be the perspective of a changed world, and thus by changing it now you are changed now. In a perfect world, we will only see perfection. Therefore, we can live in a perfect world now by only seeing perfection. This is Social transformation through personal transformation. If it is true for you then it will be true for all and be universalized.

III

Next, we describe how the actual process of transformation occurs in an individual's life and how this translates to the individual's collective community

Chapter 30

The *Why* of "How?"

To stay consistent with the beginning chapters of the last two parts, we will now move our conversation, not immediately to a discussion about how transformation occurs, but first why it is necessary to describe the how.

Maybe there would be a proper method to describe how to describe the how or how to describe describing, and maybe this can be useful to dive into if only briefly and shallowly. Hopefully it is not too shallow of an idea that we will hit our heads on the bottom. Most things aren't. If you dive into a subject and hit your head on the bottom, you are not diving into the truly deep parts, and sometimes it is necessary to move locations or change your question. It can be the same topic or same waters, just in a different place or in a different way.

Why do we describe the how? What use does asking how serve? A why without a how is just a dream and a how without a why is just a plan. The why drives your vision and the how drives the execution of that vision. Both are needed. Knowing what you want to do and how to do it are two different forms of knowledge.

Some people know what they want to do, but they have no way to do it, or so they think. Some people are really good at doing, but can find themselves running all day and getting nowhere. The why is where you want to go and the how is the way to get to where you want to go.

The how is the roadmap. Just like on many road trips we experience unpredicted detours and delays. But, if you also know how to deal with detours and delays then it is still part of the plan of the overall how to get where you want to go.

In terms of this how, explaining how the actual process of transformation occurs is one of our objectives in this part. And, explaining how this translates from the individual to the collective community is our secondary objective.

Though, with this secondary objective the ideas about how the personal world is reflected into the social world have been described previously, so in this sense we will not endeavor to repeat ourselves and give this objective its own separate chronological space, but will integrate it with the discussion on how personal transformations occur.

How personal transformations occur in general and how they will occur for each person seems to be different. We can all unite in the same why and even the same what, but the how often has to be personalized and applied according to the needs and circumstances of the individual.

However, even though the details might differ, the principles of the how are the same. Some of the differences can be accounted for by the difference between what *does* happen and what *should* happen. This *should* is always a one-way formula, but that *does* is what brings about the differences.

We will focus on the *should*. Anything that does happen that is different must be brought back into the context of the should. It is important that we all undergo the same process, because sameness yields sameness. In terms of temporal structures, we often think that you can take many paths to get to the same place. But, to get to the best place one must take the best path and there is always only one best path. And this path is the path you "should" take.

Therefore, in our way of describing how personal transformations take place, we are implying that our way of describing them is also likewise a way of prescribing how they should take place. Those who transform themselves in any other way will reach an end as different as their means.

With the idea of simplicity being the ultimate form of sophistication, we will strive to keep the process as simple as possible. If one finds that their process is too complex, they themselves are probably off the path. The true path is simple. It is the simplest, the shortest, but also the most misunderstood.

It is sometimes as easy as looking at a brass serpent or washing in a dirty river seven times. Sometimes what you do doesn't matter as much as that you do. It is true in the process of transformation that transforming itself always trumps the end to which you are transforming toward. On the journey, you must think and enjoy only the journey itself. Before you start the journey, you make your roadmap and you know where you need to go. But, on the journey you just focus on going.

The last chapter we gave the destination and here we will give the roadmap, but for you the reader and we the writers, we give all our focus and attention to the act and process of transforming itself. One must cultivate in themselves a constant awareness of the transformation that is taking place always in themselves.

In every moment, one is being pulled either towards the positive or towards the negative. The only static person is the one who has pulled themselves out of the process entirely. Once you start the journey you can never pull out. It is like climbing a rope toward the top that is burning from the bottom up underneath you. The only way to safety is up. There is no turning back.

One has the opportunity here while they are reading to be transformed. The book itself will not transform the reader, nor the words in it. Neither will we the writers be the cause or the interpreted meaning gained from the writing. The transformation starts with your choice and is completed by the completion of the choice. The progress from choice to completion is the very process of transformation itself.

How to choose and how to complete what you choose is what this part will entail. Why the how is necessary to further both our argument and our aspiration has hopefully been explained satisfactorily and can thus be trusted.

Chapter 31

What Is Transformation and How Does it Work?

Without giving a dictionary definition, we can think of transformation as when something takes a different form. The form of an object dictates in a large measure both the object's utility and its essence. These two different ways of looking at the implications of form are helpful to consider in trying to dissect what form means for people.

Utility is the pragmatic approach to understanding what something is. You can use a big kitchen bowl as a pot for your plants because it has the form of a pot. You can call a couch a bed if it is where you consistently sleep. It is the use you make of the object that forms it. This is the Hebraic way of thinking, as we discussed before.

Essence is the abstract conception of an object wherein its meaning only comes about through symbols that are shared by language. This is the platonic, or Greek way of thinking. We use our language in an attempt to describe an object, but just as we can never make the perfect object through material means, neither can our mortal tongue adequately describe an object in its perfect form. Thus, all attempts to do so are futile, and formlessness becomes a form in itself.

The pragmatic approach to form is understanding that the form an object takes will influence the role the object takes. The abstract approach to form is understanding that a material object can never represent the perfect form of the object. Thus, for an object to transform is to change from a material form into an immaterial form and thus step into a new role.

Imperfection can never yield perfection and therefore we cannot transform ourselves. We cannot take upon ourselves a form that has never been known by us. The perfect standard or form of which we are to take must exist outside of us, but is what also must work inside of us to change us to become like it.

We must essentially take on a new form and subsequently act according to the roles inherent in this new form. To transform therefore is to become what you are not now. To reform is to merely fix the current form. It is like taking a car that is bent out of shape and pounding it from the inside out to remove the dents.

However, transforming is taking all the existing material and using it to create something new and assumingly better. Sometimes, still going with the car analogy, parts can be brought in from without and a complete restoration can take place. This is restoring it to its original state, but with new parts.

With humans it is much the same, but also different. What we are becoming or being restored to is in one sense what we already were and potentially already are, but have for some reason been broken and dinged up by the experience of life. Just like a car can exist longer than the owner of the car, so does the history of mankind.

We are not just the products of our own past, but all the past pasts past, or the previous histories before. We learn things from our elders that are not true that are only taught because they were taught to our elders by their elders.

Transformation is therefore to transform back to the way things were before they became distorted and into the way things must be if they are to never be distorted again.

This is as we talked about in Part I: sustainable change. Different than a car that is restored, once we undergo our restoration and are transformed back into the new way of living, we will be undingable.

Though perfection can only exist in an immaterial state as we currently understand it, our transformed state will be a perfect unity of immateriality and materiality. Thus, perfection is possible even here. Even now.

This idea is encapsulated by other words and concepts where trans- is used. People and or Prophets past have been transfigured and or translated. They take on a new figure and are given a clean slate. This transfiguration and translation do not occur by the agent's will alone, but as is the case with transformation, the transformed must be transformed by something outside of them.

Is the transforming agent God himself or is it something he holds the power to. Is he the agent that cleans or does he have control over the cleaning agent?

We will examine this question further in the next chapter, but as to conclude this chapter we see that transformation is becoming what you are. It has been said that to become what you want to be you must be what you want to become.

To become transformed you must be transformed. Being transformed is something that happens in the present. Becoming transformed is something that happens in the presence of the transforming agent. Whether it be the agent them self or the agent of transformation held by the agent alone.

Therefore, how transformation works is dependent upon by two factors. The factors within one's control and the factors without. There are factors without that are pluralistic and there is a factor without that is singularistic. There's only one thing that ultimately transforms you, though the word *ultimately* is used in terms of chronology more than our mortal perception of majority.

It feels like we do the majority of the transforming ourselves, but that infinitely close difference between our best efforts and perfection are more than our efforts times infinity. It is this gap that is closed by the agent of transformation.

Chapter 32

Transforming Agent and Agent of Transformation

The transforming agent and the agent of transformation are two different things or non-things. Or, it might even be both. Which is which, the transforming agent or the agent of transformation, does not really matter because you can read both both ways. What does matter is that there are two separate and distinct agents involved.

The one agent speaks of an actual person being an agent. The other agent speaks of something a person would use to accomplish a given task. Such as the use we use today when we talk about cleaning agents that we use to clean specific items and/or surfaces. Is it an agent as a person cleans us or an agent as a thing that cleans us? And by cleans us we are using in a synonymous fashion as is the concept of transformation. Are we transformed by someone or something?

Remember the context of which we are speaking of transformation. This transformation that comes from something external to us is after we have done all we can in terms of the things that are within our power. This is about relying upon a power, whether it be an all-powerful person or an all-powerful thing, that is not us or something we have in our possession.

In our modern world we try to save ourselves by our own good works. This work both includes the things that we do and the things that we make. The things that we do are the fruit of who we are. The things we make are the fruits of what we do. As producers we make products. We try to save ourselves by the merits of how well of producers we are and how well our products are.

Concrete examples of both are the following:

How much of technology and modern progress has been used as an attempt to both prolong our lives and promote our current well-being. Though we might be surviving longer, are we thriving more? The types of transformations these yield are still temporal and finite. What is living a few more years compared to the option of living forever? If it is not the things that we produce that will save us, what about our merits as producers in themselves?

This is the idea that we can transform ourselves. This is an even harder idea to refute than the last one, because it deals much with things that are immaterial. We can more easily see the vain attempts of trying to save ourselves with technology, than we can see our similar vain attempts to save ourselves by ourselves. The most easy way to refute this idea is to use an idea that is also immaterial in origin and practice, but also evident as a fruit of actions. This idea is the irony of humility.

The irony of humility and how it relates to saving ourselves is that glory must be given somewhere. With what we make, we give the glory to the things we make. With what we do we give the glory to the doer. Humility is deferring the glory to someone or something else. It can be a sign of humility to give the glory to a technology. It can be a sign to give the glory to another person, but if that person is part of the collective transformation effort then they cannot accept the glory either. Therefore glory floats waiting to be claimed.

This is why something or someone external to the individual and external to the collective must exist. And, this someone or something cannot have its existence be dependent upon by either the individual or the collective or indirect glory could be given to the same. In fact, the relationship of dependency goes in reverse. The ideal glory-giving scenario would be to give glory to the being or the thing that made the scenario possible.

This goes back to the agent of transformation and the transforming agent. Just as this agent transforms the agents both individually and collectively in the end, it is also the same agent that made the same agents in the beginning be able to transform in the first place.

Therefore, the transforming agent is not something or someone involved only at one time in the process of transformation, but has been, is, and will be involved throughout the process of transformation. Even when transformation has its end and is complete, the transforming agent's role is endless and never complete. This is because whatever transforms is transformed and continues to transform as the transformed continue to transform.

Once transformed, new transformed agents will begin transforming agents themselves. And, the transforming agent will continue as they were because transforming agents is part of who they are. Thus, this cycle and progression has both an end in one aspect and is endless in another.

Now back to the question whether it is the agent as a person or the agent as a thing that actually transforms. And, why does it even matter?

If it is a person, it is not a person like us that is under the same mortal conditions as us, but is one that has already undergone a similar transformation as we are undergoing. If it is a thing, it is not a thing that we could have made or could make, but has existed as itself as long and with as much efficacy as the transformations it makes possible and realizes.

But, what if it is both? What if the agent of transformation is the embodiment of the transforming agent it uses and possesses. What if the person's identity is the personification of the endless, all-powerful, immaterial thing? And, if as a person they have an end in themselves, their power is self-contained, and their materiality is as real as is their personhood. They blend with it and it blends with them.

The very transformation process for us is likewise to blend with them and thus blend with it. But, with them or it as being the higher agent in the equation, we must be invited into this realm and qualified by those of that realm to exist, live, and participate in the similar operations of the realm. It is only the realm of the transformed that makes it possible and practical for those still in the realm of the untransformed.

Chapter 33

Hierarchy of Consumption

We talked of this higher realm wherein those of the transformed dwell from which none have ever fell. Yes, we might have just used that word to make it rhyme, but now that we have used it, let us explain about the concept of falling.

With our eternal, infinite, and spiritual perspective as described in part two, we know that we existed before we exist now. The materials of which our bodies are composed are eternal and our spirits themselves are likewise. The unity of the Spirit and body is what is new for us in this life. Though, it seems to be only temporary as when we die our bodies go into the ground and our spirits leave.

The realm of the transformed is where spirit and body are united forever. With this unity in the self, unity of the society is likewise manifested. To reach this higher realm one must unite themselves in the lower realm to the best of their ability and then rely upon the transforming agent from the higher realm to complete the transforming process.

This reliance upon a higher realm to become part of the higher realm is not something new, but can be observed from merely looking at some of these similar progressions in our own world.

Starting with the lowest realm, the realm of the elements or minerals, we see that they are consumed by plants and thus become part of the plant kingdom. We then see that plants are consumed by animals and then become part of the animal kingdom.

Next, we see humans who consume both plants and animals and the very elements and minerals in these plants and animals are what make us, as it has been said, "you are what you eat." We as humans believe ourselves to be at the top of the food chain, but with our uniqueness in our capacities as humans, we also have a unique higher chain to consume us.

This higher consumer is the realm of the trans-formed. As humans in the realm of the untransformed, we have the capacity to choose. This capacity has been given to us and will not be taken from us unless we give it away. We can give it away to animal-like passions and pursuits and thus become consumed by animal-like endeavors. Or, we can give it away to something and or someone of the higher chain and thus be consumed by them. When we are consumed by them, we, like the transformation from mineral to plant to animal, become part of the higher kingdom.

This is a transformation into a higher kingdom. It is taking on a new form, as we discussed in the second chapter of this part. The form of the transformed. Those of this form do not call themselves transformed, because for them it is the only form there is. Their collective transformity is the strongest form of unity and is thus considered uniformity. What they seek uniformly is to unite the untransformed with their form and thus help to transform those of the lower form.

Those of the lower form must willingly give themselves to the higher form. In willingly giving, they give their will. Their will is all they have that is theirs and is all that is theirs to give. The higher form will not take this unwillingly because it is impossible. An unwilling will cannot exist in the realm of the willing wills. The unwilling will untransformed themselves to the lower kingdom in the likeness of the lower kingdom. The animal kingdom wherein there is no capacity to choose and thus no will.

With all this talk of transformation into higher kingdoms and or realms, we are not suggesting reincarnation. We do not know all the laws that govern the spiritual and physical realms of the lower kingdoms and even entirely of the higher kingdom. We do know the laws that are expedient for us to know to reach the higher kingdom.

The higher kingdom is what Christians call the kingdom of God. It is as much a place external, like a kingdom kingdom, as it is a place to come from internally. Those who live in the kingdom of God are of the kingdom of God. They have become new creatures by the grace of the appointed being of the higher kingdom who was their agent of transformation.

Falling, as comically expressed at the beginning of this chapter, has happened once and can happen again for those who choose it. Falling is falling to a lower kingdom. Not as literally as a noun, but moreso as a verb in the likeness of that kingdom.

Rising is rising to a higher kingdom, but in this case it is both a noun and a verb. It is a verb in that you act in the likeness of that kingdom, but is also a noun in that with the help of the transforming agent you become a literal part of that higher kingdom.

When we speak of the fall of Adam and Eve, we realize that they did not fall from the higher kingdom, because it is not possible to fall from this higher kingdom in noun. But, they fell in verb through their actions of disobedience and thus we remain today fallen in likeness and in essence or noun.

It is easy to think simply of falling as bad and rising as good, but we could never rise if we never fell. There is a concept called Anti-fragile by Nassim Nicholas Taleb, that gives the difference between bad and good falling. With something fragile, we say, "don't drop me or I'll break." Or, if the object is resilient we can say, "go ahead and drop me, I won't break."

But, anti-fragile is saying, "drop me so I break." In this last case, breaking is good because one becomes stronger as they rise from the fall. Though, the nature of the thing being dropped is not a thing. It is something organic that can both heal itself and be healed to become stronger than it was before.

It is living in an untransformed world and body that we experience all the necessary fallings that make it possible for us to rise to the new world with a new body and spirit that are as united as the society in which the individual is part. Therefore, our greatest disadvantage has become our greatest advantage.

Chapter 34

A Change of Heart

Social transformation is really the same as saying, "change the world." Personal transformation is the same as saying, "change a world" or to change your life. Changing a world starts at the heart with the heart by a change of heart.

Thus, a social transformation is parallelly a change of hearts. Or, to put it in the terms of this book, a transformation of hearts. To transform a heart is to be given a new heart. It is to change from a stony heart to a heart of flesh (Ezekiel 36:26). The old one must be removed and the new one must be put in.

Just like a heart surgeon could never give themselves a heart transplant because they would be dead the moment they took their heart out, we cannot perform the heart transplant by ourselves either. In theory, a machine could take the place of the heart while the heart transplantation is taking place and thus it is with us. We rely upon the merits not of a machine, or some other imperfect person like us, but the transforming agent. But, in more practical terms, what does this change of heart look like?

A way to both see and assess your own heart is to understand the feeling of constraint in relation to external laws.

In the perfect, transformed, changed society external laws will exist. Even though, the laws are written on the hearts of the people, internally, they still will exist. The existence of these laws is unique, because they exist not because they have to, but because they are desired. With these types of laws and the alignment of hearts to them, more freedom is found with them then without them. How does this work and what has to happen for it to work?

For a society to come from the place of not needing laws, but wanting laws, the society must undergo a transformation of sorts starting with the individuals' transformations themselves. Each individual must undergo a transformation from needing law to wanting law.

This very switch from need to want is the change of heart. Things, animals, or even people coming from an animal-like mentality and level of individual agency, always come from a place of need that is usually selfish. Humans, fully realized or fully engaged in the process of being realized, come from a place of want that is always selfless.

Law historically has been used to govern us, but in a transformed world we would use law to govern ourselves. In one case, the law acts upon the individual, while in the other case the individual acts with the law or we could say according to the law. Acting according to the law for the law itself. It is as we talked before, doing one's duty for the right reasons. Those who are acted upon by the law do not do so out of their own free will, but out of an obligation or constraint they feel they need to keep.

For them, *laws are constraining to keep, but for those who want the law; the law becomes constraining to break.*

Moral laws constrain us in these two ways and can also be classified as regulative and constitutive. When viewing moral laws as regulative the laws exist external to the person and press down upon them, regulate them, and are constraining to keep. When moral laws are viewed as constitutive the laws exist internal to the person and literally become part of the person or "constitute" them. Instead of being constraining to keep, they are constraining to break.

People in this state of nature govern themselves and no third-party person or regulative law is needed to control neither the individual nor the collective. External moral laws can be done away with, though we are not to do without them until they are within us. In our society we mistakenly seek to get rid of external moral laws prematurely because of the inherent discomfort that comes with persistent regulative constraints. Yet if they were a part of us, we would never feel such discomfort only unless we broke them.

Therefore, for those for whom morals constitute them, discomfort becomes a choice instead of a given and in this transformed state of nature we would never choose to go against our state of nature.

In terms of assessing yourself and where your heart is, you can evaluate the feelings of constraint that swell up when you are called to keep up with your duty to follow the law. If there is a good or righteous law that is hard for you to keep then you need a change of heart. If there is a good or righteous law that is hard for you to break, even with peer pressure, then your heart is probably in the right place. In this case, for the example of being peer pressured, you want for those that are pressuring you to change their hearts.

It is often ironic that the person who needs to change their heart doesn't want to and the person who would easily want to doesn't need to.

It is the very act of wanting to change one's heart that changes one's heart. The feeling of yearning to be better is a sign that you are turning better. To turn comes from the same root as to repent or to change or to transform. The act of needing only hardens the heart. This is the same for wanting or needing others to change.

When you want people to change, coming from a place of selfless love, they feel this love and it can transform them if they allow it. When you need people to change, coming from a place of demanding it, others feel forced and often turn further away from the thing you are trying to force them to turn to. In these cases, you need to change before they can ever change. Be the change you wish to see in others.

Because a change of heart is something that happens internally, it cannot be brought about by external means. But, external means can be used to see and measure the progress of the internal changes that one is making.

A change of heart is a change of the way in which we try to change hearts. In the next chapter, we will talk about how one's personal transformation can, is, and should be very connected to the transformation of others.

Chapter 35

Personal Transformation Through Social Transformations

It is a phenomenological experience of those who help others to feel that they themselves have been helped more in the process. It is from this experience that we both describe why and how it is necessary in the collective transformations of all persons, as well as it is one of the shoulds we prescribe, not only for the benefit of all, but for the benefit of the one who seeks the benefit of all.

Emanuel Levinas has described the spirit as the other-in-you. What this means is that you yourself, though separate from the other, are also inseparably connected with them. Separate in that you are you and they are they, but connected in that in the most extreme measure their wants are your needs.

In our current world, there is a typical ordering when it comes to wants and needs and pursuing them and fulfilling them with regard to both yourself and the other.

We often think that we cannot help another if we ourselves are in need of help. Therefore, our needs would go before their needs. However, the switch is that you might find your needs satisfied in the process of helping satisfy the needs of others. This is the paradox of trying to save yourself and losing yourself and by losing yourself you find yourself. But, as all arguments seem to go better when they are combined, we will do this here.

What if both ideas were true? What if it was both better to help yourself first and better to help the other first? Isn't this impossible?

Can there only be one *first*? Yes, if you look at first in the same way. But, what other types of firsts are there? There is a first in terms of time and a first in terms of focus. Maybe in time you help yourself first, but in focus you help the other first.

Focus is really the orientation of the soul. If our soul is really the other-in-you, like Levinas suggested, then we are being inauthentic as human beings when the being of our focus is ourselves and not other human beings. With a focus in orientation on the other, everything you do for you, you do for them. Time is temporal and thus chronology is not as important as priority. Thus, we can conclude that when we put another first we speak of priority, and when someone is thinking eternally, the distinction doesn't need to be made.

By helping others you help yourself and by helping yourself you can help others more. And, the more you help others the more you help yourself and the more you help yourself the more you can help others. This makes the amount of helping that could come from one, be able to help all. And, if all helped all, we would inevitably be one.

Oneness, is one of the chief characteristics of social transformation. Social transformation is a society of people who have transformed their typical orientation from themselves to others. By all doing this, they all become of one mind and of one heart and also for one mind and for one heart. And, because everything is present with them they also come from one heart and one mind. Thus, by eliminating a past of untrueness to truth, they can move past the past to true trueness.

Therefore, if transformation is the greatest need for all, then helping others in this is the greatest service you can give. And, the service always goes both ways. You are transformed as you help transform. And as you are transformed you are able to transform more those whom you help to transform.

This has been extensively researched by many leadership theorists and is commonly called the Transformative Approach to

Leadership. This approach is a process that occurs between a leader and a follower, wherein both are edified in the interaction. Thus it is essential for one's own transformation to help in the transformations of others. For this reason, we describe it as personal transformation through social transformations.

The social, meaning in this case, the other. The other is the you that is not you. It is youness, but not you yourself. You yourself will always be your self and they themselves will always be their own self. You yourself and they them self together become us ourselves. This is the social. Ourselves can mean two or it can mean all. But, though we use the plural, "social transformations" in this case the plural is less. Because in this case, social transformations is ourselves as two.

Social transformation is ourselves as all. Therefore, social being a plural word itself is multiplied by the plural word transformations and as two negatives make a positive, two plurals make a singular social encounter. And, with social transformation, social is plural and transformation is singular, and as a negative and a positive always make a negative, so does a plural and a singular always make a singular.

It helps to see this better when we switch the order of the words. The encounter of two social beings would be the transformations of socials (meaning two people engaging in a social interaction) and the encounter, occurrence, and or phenomena of all social beings would be the transformation of society (meaning all the social beings that make up that society). All who are not social would not be part of the society, because socializing is societing (verb). And, true society is always both the noun and the verb.

As social beings, we must be social to be true to who we are. And, the most important social activity we can engage in when it comes to the most important outcome we are seeking, is helping to transform the other and thus each other.

Therefore, those who do not have the orientation of the soul to the other are not truly being social and therefore are not truly of the society of the transformed. And, will never reach the realm of the transformed either until they themselves change themselves. If they are the only ones unchanged, all the changed will put their focus on them.

But, the truly changed know that focus on a person does not force a person. And, it is ultimately up to the person themself to enforce this orientation of mind and heart to the other for themselves.

Chapter 36

Personal Transformations through Social Transformation

As hinted at in the last chapter, we will now talk about how one's personal transformation is tied up with their quest for social transformation. This being a necessary part of their quest as individuals, it is also a necessary part collectively for individuals. Thus, all persons share in common the destination of social transformation and share in the journey as well.

We will show that one personally transforms when they help to socially transform the world. And, how a socially transformed world helps create fertile soil for the seed of personal transformation to grow and go with quickness and quality.

First, how does one personally transform when they seek to transform the social. This is a lesson I learned from my own life. I had given to me the perfect learning experience that came in the form of a physical ailment. As I sought treatment for this ailment, it occurred to me one day that the only way to feel better physically was to be better spiritually. Trying to do certain spiritual acts that helped me feel better spiritually were not enough, I needed to be better spiritually. The difference between doing and being is what complete transformation sums up.

I began my journey of personal transformation initially for my own well-being; thinking that once I was well I could then go on and do everything I ever wanted to do with my life, including helping others. I realized, however, that my own complete personal transformation was dependent upon the self-made conditional idea of helping others. I say helping others was conditional in my mind because for me it was, "if I am doing good myself I will do good for others." I realized that being lives in the land of unconditionality and therefore I could never be good myself without being good to others.

There is always a concomitant relationship between helping yourself and helping others. As we talked about in the last chapter, our focus should be on others alone, even if the chronology or appearance of help looks self-interested. Though, the difference between the helping others of this chapter is the context in which we help others.

Last chapter, we talked about helping others one-by-one through their own personal transformations and thus bringing about social transformation. Here, we are talking about helping all as if one through one social transformation or even one collective personal trans-formation. A personal transformation in the view of looking at society as one person.

Wanting to help others was my desire and my words at that time were, "I want to change the world." The world is thus social transformation. A world is social transformations or collective personal transformations. I had this big focus that I wanted to change the entire world. Just as people must have a focus on helping the one, or the individual, we must also maintain the focus of helping all, the one society of which all are part of.

I realized the relationship between helping all and helping myself when one day it occurred to me stronger than a fleeting thought, but as a hard-pressed impression on my soul that, *"the lessons I learned from changing my world would be the lessons the world needs me to teach to change it."* I believe this is true for all, for what is intimately personal is absolutely universal.

The experiences we gain in our lives are not by accident. We do not earn them ourselves, but each experience, as each moment, is a gift. Experiences are given to us not only for us, but for all. As we experience the process of changing our own worlds, we learn what we need to teach to change the world.

Thus we see many people who overcome great odds teaching, motivating, and inspiring others to overcome the odds in their own lives. This is one of the best ways of determining what your calling in life is. By examining what you have been called to go through in the past, you can understand how to go through the process of creating your future.

You might find people who have gone through similar things and therefore you can share in this common experience and share your experience with others who are experiencing what you as a group have all experienced. All who have experienced the same thing did not learn the same things. Thus, someone who is experiencing the same thing might not need to learn what you learned, but what someone else learned. Or, in most cases, they will learn something completely new and different and thus your teaching doesn't teach them the thing they need to learn, but prepares them for it.

Joining with others in your pursuit to help others is what we call an organization. It is an organization that is social in nature because it is more than one person. And, this organization's mission is likewise social in nature, in that it intends to help no less than all it is meant to help. Thus comes the unified effort to change the world. And, those unified are united in a common cause that will not cause to change the world or socially transform it.

As they succeed, they will find that the more the social world becomes transformed, the more personally-transformed people there are. Obviously, in the first place because it was the personal transformations of the people that make up the social transformation, but also in another way. It is the social transformation itself that creates a better environment for personal transformations to occur. And, given a better environment, more people will choose to accept the invitation to transform themselves or excel quicker in their process of transforming themselves.

It is not the environment that changes anyone, but it is everyone who changes the environment that creates the environment for change to occur. They cannot create change themselves or cause it in any way, but they can change the environment, which includes the society or the social world in which others live.

As others learn and grow and transform themselves, they will not have to repeat the lessons that those before them should have learned, but will rise with those before them to learn higher lessons, reach higher ground, and be closer each day to the higher realm.

Chapter 37

Habits and Culture—
Doing and Becoming

Aristotle said, "We are what we repeatedly do." What you repeatedly do is what we commonly call a habit. The difference between doing and being (being is synonymous with "is and are") seems to be tied up somehow with consistency. The quote could also read, "you consistently do what you are."

People sometimes say, "you are not what you do." Though true, you are what you consistently do. One act of wrongness does not make you a wrong person, but wrong people tend to consistently do wrong acts. The art of becoming is consistently doing that which you want to become. Or, as has also been said before, "you become what you want to be by being what you want to become." *Being* in the second half of this quote suggests consistent doing.

A habit is a pattern of action. And action does not always have to be external, but can be internal acts such as the choices and inward commitments one makes to themselves and or God. A true commitment is a true change, because if it is not, it was not truly made.

The process of consistently doing is a process of making commitments. As one makes commitments, one often breaks them. But, as one keeps them one breaks away from the old way of being and is thus transformed into a new being. Transforming is synonymous with becoming. Being is synonymous with transformed.

A habit is something you are individually. Culture is something we are collectively. Culture is merely the external habits of individuals, and habits are the internal cultures of the collective.

Like all things collective or social, culture is something that is shared. People can have many different habits, but collectively, they can only have one culture. This one culture is the one collective habits of a society. And, within the society as a whole are many different societies with many different cultures.

What we all share are what we consider to be cultural universals. Total and true social transformation will be a complete and comprehensive sharing of culture. All cultures will become one culture and one culture will be universal. There will be no need to speak of cultural universals, because that will be all that there is. Those who are not of the culture are not of the same universe and thus they do not break the universal standard, but are broken by it. They are broken off from it by their own choice or lack of choice which is a choice in itself.

Those who choose to be part of the culture will by their choice make their first universal commitment, which is a commitment to choose. All people who are in this culture share the value of choice and therefore it will be a culture of choice and of agency.

To become this culture collectively, we must develop the habits of choice individually. One's ability to choose is the greatest gift given to us, but is also the greatest responsibility for us. As we become responsible individually, we will create first within ourselves a habit of responsibility that will then translate collectively into the same, though as a culture of responsibility. Thus, coupled with the culture of agency is the culture of responsibility.

These two cultural universals must be the first two to be accepted by the collective or the society. It is because these two habits are what allow for the process of forming and conforming to the rest of cultural universals that will be given to us and for us.

It is by choice we commit and by responsibility or accountability we stay true to our choice or commitment. Without the shared values, a society could never stay true to itself. Without these values on an individual level, a person can never be true to them self.

We then see that the becoming, changing, and transforming happens individually as one develops new habits. And, the becoming, changing, and transforming happens collectively as all develop culture. It is the people who transcend old habits and become new people that change the world. They change the world by changing themselves and by changing themselves they create within themselves a new culture; a higher culture that calls others up to it by merely being what it is.

These people of the higher culture are the ones who can preach a sermon without saying a word. It is a society of these people that will make the world what it could be, and those who resist these people are what make the world what it should not be or what it currently is.

As the world transforms, new shared habits will emerge that will shape the culture of the world. Those who just go with the flow will conform to the new social norms and thus start acting consistently in a way that is higher. Thus, by acting consistently in a higher way, they become higher themselves. Maybe there is less merit to people who fall into the higher realm, but if they are to stay there, they must one day make the conscious choice to stay.

Therefore, anyone who is lifted up must still hold their own weight. And, all who lift up are given strength to carry the weight of the world with ease. For truly they are yoked up with something or someone bigger and stronger than themselves. Their goal is the goal of the great goalie who stands at the gate of the realm of the transformed.

Chapter 38

Becoming Together

Because culture is social in nature, its transference from one person to another happens in context of social interaction. It is been said by Frederick Nietzsche, though paraphrased, that "culture cannot be taught, but must be imparted by encounters with the exemplar."

Who you are with seems to relate with who you are. Obviously, this does not include surface-level material relationships. For example, a rich person who spends his time ministering to the poor might never become poor in a material sense, but might just become poor in spirit. This poorness in spirit is part of the transformation of self.

There is both negative and positive peer pressure. Negative peer pressure comes from those less transformed who try to *lessen* those who are more transformed. Positive peer pressure comes from those who are more transformed trying to *"moren"* those who are less transformed. Though transformation, as is the same with righteousness, is a choice, one choice that is helpful to make is who you let influence your choices.

In an untransformed state, one is not all conscious all the time. Therefore, they that can be swayed by the winds of group dynamics can find themselves doing what they themselves would not do if they were alone. Now, this could have good consequences. If others inspire and encourage you to act in a way that is more transformed, then this is good, but if others encourage you to do bad or discourage you from doing at all, then this is bad. The good will never have to discourage you from doing or acting, at least not implicitly. The truly good will always be up to something truly good, thus by joining with them you are also enjoining with them in their pursuits.

Thus, if one is to transform themselves it is helpful to spend time with and around those who help to transform you. Spending time with these people is never an expense, but always an investment. However, for the investment to truly work you will not enter the relationships with the cost-benefit mentality, but to see the relationship as an end in itself.

With these true principles, comes the risk of misunderstanding. It would be a very untransformed way of thinking to only involve yourselves with transformed people. If everyone always tried to find someone better than them, then no one would ever be able to be friends with anyone, because relationships in their true nature must be two-way.

The best person on earth could not associate with anyone due to everyone's status below them, yet it is truly the "best of the best" that often seek the most to help the "worst of the worst." This is why Jesus spent most of his time with sinners.

But, if it is well for the untransformed to seek the company of the transformed and it is natural for the transformed to want to be with the untransformed and help them, then this relationship would seem to work well. In some cases, this is so. But, this is still all too simplistic. Let's dive further.

Up until now, we have been looking at people as nouns. But what if, we started looking not at the people's status, but what they are stating with their actions. The best way for an untransformed person is to start acting in a transformed way. Thus, when they go to surround themselves with transformed people, they must participate in transforming people. There is no hanging out in the realm of the transformed, but only service.

It has been said that service doesn't get you to heaven, but is the way of heaven. Just being with transformed people doesn't transform you, but doing with them what they do. Thus, in your friend search you are not going around and judging people as better or worse than you in that you are trying to avoid the bad and pursue the good.

You pursue the good by pursuing good. When you are pursuing good you will find others who are pursuing good too. And, it is those who are pursuing good who are presumably the good people you are seeking. Therefore, you find good people by being a good person. You only find bad people by finding the bad in people and this is why it is safer to stay away from looking at people as nouns, instead of looking at the verbs they do.

You come to be most strongly tied with those whom you become with. You become better individually as you help others to become and you become better socially as you engage socially with others who are becoming too. Therefore, there is a social aspect of becoming and it is often referred to as growing together.

This is why husbands and wives raising children often become so close to each other, because they are engaged in the activities of helping children become better. The husband and wife, through this process of helping others become better, become better themselves personally, but also together as well. They become a better team because they become as one.

Therefore, if we as a world are to become as one, we must all become engaged in the process of becoming both personally and socially. If we neglect to become with others, we will eventually only be with ourselves. Thus we must grow alone and grow together simultaneously.

It is like the roots of the great redwoods. They grow tall independently, but underneath the surface their roots are bound together holding each other up, allowing each other to grow taller and stronger than if they were on their own. Thus it is with transformation. You personally transform more if you transform socially together with other persons. As you become better together, you become together better.

Therefore, to be better you don't have to surround yourself with people who are better, just with people who are striving to be better just as you. It's less important who is better and more important who is bettering. You will not be measured by the altitude you reach, but by the growth you make. The difference between where you started and where you end, is the greatest difference you can make.

Chapter 39

Gift and Exchange

To give an example of what a transformed life and a transformed society would look like, we will compare two modes of transference of goods and services as both gifts and exchange. We will examine these two in the context of personal and impersonal relationships.

We will seek to describe the ideal in order to give a clear measure for which to strive. We know the society and modes of transference in which we suggest are possible, because most of us will understand it. We will understand it because we have either done it or have had it done to us at one time. And, if it can be done once, it can be repeated. Like it is with consistent action, by repeatedly acting in the ways prescribed, one will become the ideal and be the embodiment of it.

There will be four categories we will explore. Personal gifts, personal exchange, impersonal gifts, and impersonal exchange. We will see that where society is is not where it should be and where it should be is where it could be and for some people already is.

It is a way of life for some, but for a full social transformation to occur, it must become the way of life for all. I myself can only speak of it because I am not there. Though, by speaking of it I become more committed to it, the more I see myself through the lens of these ideal types and learn their implications.

We will start with impersonal exchange because it is what our modern world knows and practices so well. It is not necessarily something wrong, but something to be aware of. Though, the opposite of it, personal gifts, seems to have something extra right about it.

Impersonal exchange has been an unintended consequence of an ever-growing society. As societies grow there are more people to know and thus more people to not. It is the not knowing where the impersonal comes from. To become more personal one must seek to know more persons. Every person more one knows, the more knows that one person about every person or all people.

Because our society is so big and we realistically cannot know every person on a deep and personal level, we will not be blamed for not knowing everyone as such. But, we will not be praised either for not trying to get to know everyone.

Impersonal relationships are the common-found story reiterated throughout descriptions of bureaucracy. When you deal with the government, or their workers, it is as if you are dealing with the same. The worker tries to be so impersonal as if merely they are the government working through them. Thus, it seems as if sometimes you are talking to an object rather than a person. Though this is not without exceptions, it seems to be a good illustration as to the point of impersonality.

Though, this impersonality in one sense can be expected because of the mere quantity of people a government worker is expected to deal with on a daily basis. And not only the amount of people they are to deal with, but also the amount of peopleness each person potentially brings. Peopleness is when people are people and not objects. In an impersonal relationship the ideal would be that both people be impersonal. But, sometimes one person is impersonal and the other is personal, or acting as a person and not an object.

When a person becomes personal, another person tends to want to be with this person person-to-person, but in cases where the worker person is alienated from themselves in a bureaucratical job, they are expected to be impersonal no matter what. It is because if they were to be persons to all people who came in, there would be chaos and no structure. But, when they are impersonal to all that come in, there seems to be structure, but no compassion.

Compassion is a difficult gift to give, because if and when it is given, all begin to demand its giving. Thus it is easier not to give at all. Thus, impersonal relationships and organizations tend to stick with a more exchangeable currency. This is what exchange is.

Exchange is not a gift, but is two-way; though we will find soon that gift is much more two-way then one would think. But, on the surface a gift is always one-way and an exchange is always reciprocal. You scratch my back, I'll scratch yours.

This is how the Western world operates. Trade, buy and sell, cost and benefit. We often use visible symbols such as money to measure the honesty of the exchanges. An honest exchange will be an equal exchange. Though, in our competitive world men seek to engage in the act of exchanging, but not hold up to the ideal of equal exchange.

People always want more than they give and they do this by taking more than they give. People in the gift mentality always give more than they take, but ironically they always also get more than they give. They get not by taking, but by being taken care of by the great Giver of All. This great Giver will often work through others to give the true givers their unmerited though just desserts.

People in the exchange mentality try to get more than they give and thus their fault of priority in this case might be their priority fault to work on that affects all cases in their lives.

Gift and exchange is at the root because of its connection with the ideals of selfishness and selflessness. Exchange lives in a Hobbesian world based on self-interest. Gift lives in another world, which we would suggest is the ideal world based on love and unselfishness. In the ideal world, it is not only gift giving that will define it, but the personal relationships between the gift givers and the gift getters.

In the society, one would take the time to develop a personal relationship with any person and relative proximity. Because a true gift giver gives their love unconditionally, their compassion is not bound up by some external agency, but is bound by their internal agency to give in service to others. They know the person enough to know when not to give, but they also allow themselves to know the person enough to give. And, not only allow themselves, but are allowed by the society or organization in which they assume a larger identity.

IV

Lastly, we will discuss both the urgency and importance of the promulgation of these ideas into the world and into the lives of those who are building the foundations for the future

Chapter 40

The *Why* of This *Why*

Urgency and Importance

As we have started each new part, we will start this part with a chapter devoted to the why of this why. Why is it important to discuss importance and why do we see it urgent to discuss urgency?

With the advent of all sorts of new ideas, comes to question their practicality and their endurance. With the ideas we have expressed so far we both see them as very practical and long enduring. In fact, they are so practical that we have been practicing them long before our time and are so enduring that they are eternal. The implications are infinite and their application is spiritual.

The question as to why is discussing importance important is the same as asking why to discuss why. We have already answered this, but now we will seek to answer in a different way.

When something is important, we value it. When we value something, we make it a priority. This is how we order our lives. Before we order our lives, we order all of the factors that make up our lives. Our lives are both personal and social.

The issues we have discussed have both personal and social implications. When we say that they are important, we mean that they should be given a priority and given the proper value due in order to order us as a society both individually and collectively and bring about the desired goal of social transformation.

When something is urgent, we do not have to value it, but we do have to give attention to it. The more urgent it is, the more it draws our attention. Therefore, it can become a priority, but only as a temporary one. The difference between urgency and importance here is tied up in understanding this difference in what type of priority it is.

Urgency is not something that is eternal, but temporary and temporal like we said. Urgency implies that if intervention is not made, that which is important to us will somehow be affected. Therefore, importance is at the root of what is urgent to us, but urgency is not always a necessary demand for the true merit of an important thing.

We often get lost and distracted in and out urgently trying to meet the demands of things that aren't even important to us. This can be described as being all things to all people, but when we understand what is important to us and what is important for all, we realize that we don't have to be all things to all people, but only help all people to be all things for themselves and others. And when others are all things for others, they are really just helping others to be all things for others, but not being the all thing for them.

We see therefore that importance and urgency are linked, but not directly causal. Just because something is important, doesn't mean it is urgent and just because something is urgent, doesn't mean it is important. Stephen Covey does a great job at explaining this concept in his book, Seven Habits of Highly Effective People. But, what do we hope to gain from talking about it here that a reading of his work alone would not give you, the reader?

Our discussion on the importance and urgency of these issues is twofold. One, we believe that the concepts we have discussed are very important and of eternal significance. It is because of their eternal significance that we see the temporary urgency of applying them.

Our mortal life is such a short time when compared to eternity and how we live here determines in great measure how we will live there (*there* being wherever one considers there to be.) There, or what comes next, is always dependent on what is now. To hear one beating a drum, one only hears one beat a time, but it is the beats before that that give the next beat their context.

Once one has heard the beat of eternity, they can see when they are off beat. When offbeat, it is not only important to get on beat, but also urgent.

True social transformation is being on beat with the higher realm. Because social entails more than one, we must all be in harmony with it and with each other. A whole society could be on beat with each other, but be offbeat with eternity, but when everyone is on beat with eternity everyone is on beat with each other.

Therefore, our individual missions are to personally transform ourselves and get on beat first for ourselves with eternity, the higher realm, or the transformed self. Then, when we are all one with this, we will all be one with each other.

Therefore, our important task is not to bring peace to the world, but to bring the world to the great source of peace or the "Prince of Peace". To the great "I Am" or great reality of the universe. This is important and eternity depends on it. And because eternity depends on it and our time is short here, it is also urgent.

Therefore, we will discuss what exactly is important to do and which of these things are urgent to do.

Chapter 41

What Is Important and What Is Urgent?

That which is important is everything of which we have written. Obviously, we would not have wasted the space describing anything unimportant. Now, equally as obvious, we see it as very important to us and claim it is important to all. But, only you can decide for yourself if it is important to you yourself and or everyone else.

Thus, the most important thing first is to find out if what we claim to be important is actually important. Therefore, we could have titled this chapter "How to Find what is Important", for this is truly what is important first.

If we are to create an orderly society, we must have an order of importance. Because all we can do is suggest what this order be, one must find out for themselves if this order is the right order for things to be. Therefore, we are really on a quest to find out what is right. For what is right is important.

Therefore, the first two important things one must do is find out how to find out what is important, and second how to know what you have found out is right. And, even to find out if the journey we prescribe is the right journey to find the right way.

It's with all this introductory talk, that we are digging too deeply into the issue, but that itself is the very issue. We can ask, "How do you know that that which you say is actually important?" And then, we could give a reason as to why we believe what we believe. But, then you could ask, "How do you know what you believe is actually right?" And then, we could give our explanation as to how we came to know what we believe. And this leads to one of the central problems in claiming any true knowledge. Can you know what you merely believe?

To know is not the exact same thing as believing or else we would not need to separate words. If this is so, what is the difference? And, why is this difference important in regards to our discussion on what is important here? Our main claim is that we don't just believe our main claim, but we know what we have claimed is true not only for us, but true for all. How can we know this?

Anyone can claim to know something is true at least for them, but if we are truly more than just any one person, then what is true for one should be true for all and vice versa. Therefore, we seek a universal truth, and when we find what has been true for us, we must be able to generalize it to be true for all.

Before belief comes the desire to believe. Before desire to believe, we could say one must need the desire to desire to believe and we could go on forever with a chain of desires. But eventually, desire springs forth from non-desire. Not negative desire, but non-desire. Non-desire might seem like nothingness, but as we know from one of Newton's most basic laws; no thing can come from nothing. Therefore, if non-desire is not nothing what is it?

To see two negatives, one can flip it to a positive, and therefore we must conclude it is at least a something. But, is it more than a something, meaning could it be an everything? It is probably both. Desire, belief, and knowledge all come from the same thing which is everything. Independent of each other they all come from parts that are independent of the one thing and are therefore something in themselves. But, though they are independent, their independence is dependent also in itself on the independence of which it itself is a part.

Therefore, true desire, true belief, and true knowledge are one thing. Truth. It is not possible to truly believe something that is not true while still being true to the truth from which the truth seeker came from. When one is not true to this truth, they cannot be true to any truth and therefore can never truly desire, truly believe, nor truly know anything. Because they cannot know anything, they will often be the first to claim they know everything.

Though we say what we claim here to be true, we do not claim to know the truth of all things. But, we can truly claim to have a true claim on this, the claim that true social transformation can only occur through collective personal transformations. We not only know this is true, but we also believe it is true. And, we also desire its truth to be made known and believed to all. Therefore, we see our task of promulgating these ideas to be of great importance. And, what of the urgency?

The urgency comes from knowing that to know the truth is to truly know the truth of true knowledge and what it means to those who don't believe or desire it.

The urgency comes from a desire for others to know and believe what we claim to know and believe. *The urgency is for others to see as important what we see as important.* Why it is important will be discussed, not in the getting-nowhere nonspecific "why is importance as a concept important?" but actually talking about the practical implications of our ideas and showing how and why they are important and urgent in this our day to be adopted by those who are reading this, not reading this, and anyone who is in between or outside of these two qualifiers.

You will find that you will find that by wanting to believe they are important, actually believing they are important, and claiming to know they are important, you will know, believe, and want others to know and believe that they are important too. Thus, to know everything about our claim you must first start by knowing one thing about it and that is that it is true.

You cannot know it's true until you believe it's true and you will not believe it is true until you want to believe it and you will not want to believe it until you know that it is even possible to know anything for sure. And that's why we claim that yes! You can know something, anything, and everything for sure with absolute surety and that is most important.

Now that you know you can know, what should you know?

Chapter 42

What You Need to Know

Need for our purposes here will be used synonymously with *should*. That which you should know, you need to know. And, now that you know that you *can* know, now the question is *what* to know. What to know is what is right.

Rightness implies ethics which implies things that should be followed and need to be followed if we are to live in a transformed world. Just as though what-to-knows are universal, so is the process of learning how to know what to know.

Therefore, you need to know: one, that you can know; two, how to know; and three, what to know. Since that you can know and what to know has already been prescribed in previous chapters, the focus is then turned towards how to know what is being professed to be as true is actually true. And, then to trust that truth can be found.

We make and remake this point because so much of the world is deceived in two ways. One, they think they have found true truth, when in reality they have only found part or the illusion of truth. Two, some think there is no way to know anything for sure and therefore even question their existence.

One philosopher, Descartes, only validated his existence because he realized that his thinking self was proof of his existence in his famous quote, "I think therefore I am." This, however, is in reverse in that we are or we exist independent of our thinking capacity. Our minds have just been given to us to connect the unthinking substance of spirit with the thought responding substance of body.

Science, through its empirical pursuit of knowledge using the senses, proclaims the truth in part, but only in part. It is because it only uses part of the faculties given to man. To find the full truth, you must embark on a journey led by the spirit and approved by the body. You don't prove truths through experiments, but through experience.

This is the process to know whether or not the ideas suggested in this book are true. See if they make sense on a spiritual level and then with your body of five senses go out and test them in the real world. As Jesus said, "If any man will do his will, he shall know of the doctrine" (John 7:17). It is by experimenting upon so-called true principles that you can gain an experience that will allow you to call them truly so as they really are.

Therefore, what is right has been given. You have the privilege to know what is right. Now you must act and see for yourself if these things are not true.

If they are, they will obviously be important. If important and not practiced, the need to help people to practice them will be urgent. But, why so urgent? Couldn't we just go on inching forward in progress toward eventual social transformation? Yes, we could, but why shouldn't we.

When you have come to a true knowledge of a principal, the more you procrastinate its application, the less powerful it will be for you and for others. The very fact that you are reading this book or any book that has truth in it, gives you the responsibility to not only read and be acted upon, but go out and write your own proof through your actions in the real world. The longer you wait, the more reduced will be the outcomes. And, by knowing and not doing, you will also be held more responsible for all the good you *could have* done had you acted upon what you knew.

It is this procrastinating nature of man that has led to slow and almost insignificant true social progress. On the converse, it seems as if the negative transformations are acting quickly in the opposite direction. Therefore, there lies the urgency in moving in the positive direction.

Not as if it is a competition, but an act of compassion. The more light you have, the more you can help others to see. How sad of a tale it would be if you could have seen and lightened the path for another, but chose to wait while they chose to act in a direction and on principles that were contrary to what you know to be true.

In the negative direction, people can only think to know something is true. Therefore, when you have a perfect knowledge of the truth, you are already held at a higher standard to help persuade the thinkers and help them know.

The collective need for urgency is just as urgent as is the importance of finding out what's important. We will not know whether or not we have truly done enough until we have truly felt the despair of never being able to do enough. If we think we have done enough, we are probably not doing enough. When we think we are not doing enough to help bring about good, we are probably right. But, in this feeling of not doing enough, we prepare ourselves enough to merit the receiving of the future feeling of having done all we could.

This is not just about avoiding future regret, but embracing the present opportunity. The opportunity passes the moment you pass it. Once you pass it, it will never come back to you the same. Therefore, it is important to be urgent and urgent to know what is important and to act on what it is you know and to help others to come to know for themselves too.

Anything that is justifiably not urgent is probably also not important in the true sense of true importance and true urgency.

Chapter 43

Promulgation—How to Share

In the section heading for Part 4, we used the word *promulgation* to describe the way in which we envision these ideas to go forth. To promulgate literally means to publicly cause to come forth. It is similar to promote. When we promote something there is a cause behind the promotion that causes us to want to promote it.

Therefore, when it comes to publicly causing something to come forth, it goes in two directions. We are causing one thing to go forth to all the public, but the public is also causing it to come forth for themselves. It is not as practical for us to share it with all the world, but is not as powerful either. Each person who is converted to these ideas becomes the new base point for the start of the movement in their lives. We might be the start for you, but will not be the start for all. Directly at least.

Indirect is not any less powerful of a contact. In fact, it can be a sign of an even more powerful message when those who are receivers of the message become the messengers to others. This transference from hearer to speaker is one way to measure the success of an idea.

When it comes to social transformation, there are many things that will need to be expressed to people, between people, and through people. To start with, the start is for you the reader to make readers of others.

It is our responsibility to refine the ideas enough that people will want to share them, but it is people's responsibility to share them if the ideas themselves are to refine them. Refining is what the transformation process is all about. If an idea helps you in any way, it is selfish to hold it in and not to share. With an idea, there is no fear for scarcity, because it can never run out. It only appears to run out when people disappear and run out on it.

If an idea is not true, then by all means don't just let it run out, but run away from it. If an idea is true, then run to it and then run with it. By running with it, you will find that it will begin to run you. It will fuel you. It will carry you. That is the ideal. If the idea is good enough, then it will be enough alone. It doesn't need any one person to carry it, because it can carry all. Therefore, sharing it is really not a responsibility, but a privilege.

When you share it, it will share with you more of its refining power. As you tell it, you will begin to tell that it has changed you. You must share it for you and your own personal transformation. And it must be shared for its sake alone in order to transform the lives of the sharers.

As you share it for you and it is shared for it, you and it will become one. And when you become one with it, you become one with all who are one with it. Part of its nature is to be sharing and expanding. It is because its nature is as light and light will emit its rays in all directions unless impeded.

The only person that can impede it is you, but the person your impeding will hurt most is you, too. In the end, all who seek it will find it and all those who do not share it will lose it.

The best way to share it, is to embody it. The truth that social transformation can only occur through collective personal transformations is embodied in both a perspective and an attitude towards the social world.

One's perspective must always be infinitely large and infinitely small. One must see every action they take as having eternal consequences for the future in the present. One must see and believe that they are part of a part of a part of a part that is together a whole lot greater than the whole of the parts. They must see the synergistic nature of society while at the same time seeing the unity of it. They see the potential of one-and-one making infinitely more than two, but they also see an infinite amount of components added together always summing to one.

Oneness is attained by becoming one with the realm of the transformed and synergy comes from every one being one with this realm. As these people of oneness work together, they bring others to oneness with them in ways that are more powerful than either of them could do alone.

They will personally bring forth more trans-formations as they socially bring forth more trans-formations. This is teamwork within the work team. The team is anyone engaged in the same work. Teamwork will come naturally as a result of each individual being engaged in the work. For, the work itself includes the necessity of being on the same team with all. Sharing in a common mission will help in the mission to share and thus you will share your mission in two ways both with the recruiters and the recruits.

It is not just sharing what you do, but sharing the opportunity to do what you do. With true sharing, you always leave the other with something. With this, the something is an idea and a call to act. The momentum you come into an encounter with will move them as a pendulum and they will begin to move too. Unless stubborn, you can share your energy. But, unlike objects, your energy is self-generated and expands as you give it. Therefore, as you share you will have more to share. As you move others, you yourself will move more. And, the only question now is who to share with?

Chapter 44

With Whom to Share

It is obvious that this message needs to be shared with everyone, but who in specific needs to hear this message more than anyone else. For whom is it more important that they not only receive this message, but receive it sooner than later. The message is important and urgent in itself, but the question here is who is it most important and urgent for now?

It is most important and urgent to get this message to those who give out messages regularly and influentially. We are first to share it with the sharers. If we share it with them, then they can share it with all.

This can range from the micro level to the macro level. From parents to politicians. From the corner market to mass media. But, if it encompasses all then what is the point of specificity? Aren't we all sharers in some way?

Yes, whether we like it or not we are constantly sharing both visible information and invisible transformation with everyone and anyone in which we interact. We share information by verbal or nonverbal gestures and we share transformation just by being or not being present with someone. Therefore, the question of who to share it with can really be a question of with whom do you already share interactions.

We often think of getting a new idea and taking it out to the world, when in reality the best idea would be to take it into our world. This is changing the world from the inside out. You start from within your own community and go out from there. You do not try to change what is out there first, because you cannot really change anything externally greater than it has already been changed internally. The same rule or order is what must be followed in terms of sharing.

Therefore, the first person to share it with is the next person you interact with and the next person you interact with will be the first person they share it with. You share it with them and they share with you, because when it is truly shared it is not a one-way direction, but a two-way experience.

When you are truly sharing this message, both parties, including you, will be transformed and thus you share a moment of transformation together. Then, they being more transformed then they were before the interaction, will go out into the world and share this transformation with the world and the cycle continues.

You share experiences of transformation every time you share an experience at all. It is not the sharing of an experience such as in a "show and tell," but is the sharing of an experience such as in "come and try for yourself." The message is validated by the mere fact that messaging is occurring.

When you go and tell people that social transformation can only occur through personal transformations ,you are having a social experience that is different because you are different because of what you personally have become. Therefore, just by you being you with them, you are socially transforming your relationship with them whenever you are with them.

You will notice that when you act differently, others act differently and thus through your personal actions you have changed the actions of your social environment.

Since we are all sharers, you can share this with anyone. But, you cannot share it with everyone. You do not share it with someone who is not with you to share it with. You cannot share it with someone who isn't there. The key is then to be there with people and for people by being who you are as an ever-transforming agent of transformation.

As you share it more, you will be called on to share it more. Not only in the amount of times you share it, but also in the amount of influence your sharing it has. Both quantity and quality are given to those who give themselves to each concept in their proper order. The quality of the message you share can be no greater than the quality of the messenger. That is that you cannot transform any social situation more than is your personal situation transformed.

People try to skip to quantity when they get excited by sharing new things with anyone and everyone, but we are not asking you to get excited. We are asking you to give your excitement a channel of action that leads to the actions that truly lead to something that is actually worth getting excited about. To get excited about an idea is not nearly as exciting as the realization of the idea. All the energy should then be put towards the realization of the idea and the idea of this book is both your own self-realization and the realization of the world.

Therefore, by containing your urge to share it for quantity's sake alone, you become more qualified to share it to a more broad quantity of people than you ever could have imagined. One way has the illusion of quickness, while the other has the illusion of slowness, when in reality, deliberate and careful slowness is the only way to be truly quick.

Therefore, in a way we are asking you to be nonurgent in your urgency in that you follow the curriculum yourself before you ask others to follow it themselves. Once you follow it, who you are alone will ask others to follow it for you. You will know you are not following it truly if people try to follow *you*.

You are not the idea that is being spread, but are the vessel of the idea. When a house is built, you do not give glory to the tools themselves, but to the toolers of the tools. You might glory in the building, but it is the builders that built the building that stand always more glorious, no matter how glorious the building might seem to be.

Therefore, our next questions are, "Who are the builders?" "Who is the builder?" And, "What is being built?"

Chapter 45

The Builders, the Builder, the Built

That which is being built is not really a question of what, but of who. In social transformation, we are not building anything, nor any one, but everyone.

Personal transformation is in relation to anyone, but social transformation is in relation to everyone. Therefore, in social transformation we are talking about building everyone. Who builds us then?

There are both many builders and one builder overall. The one builder is the one who built the many builders. This is the one builder in whose image we are built. It is the image of the realm of the transformed, or the image of our highest potential. Though, this builder is different in that its transformation is already complete and from an eternal perspective has always been. The transformations of the builders are being undergone. In fact, as they build they are being built.

Therefore, the builders are those who are being built and therefore those who are being built must also be builders. Builders of themselves, builders of others, and builders of they themselves and others together or society as a whole.

The executive director of the non-profit Deseret Industries once said, "Most leaders use people to build their businesses, but I use my business to build my people." The external world gives us the tools to build things in the actual external world. The tools of the internal world are the people themselves and therefore they use themselves to build the internal world of society. When this internal world has been built, the external world will have been built in the process, but only as an unforeseen consequence and not as an intentional consideration.

Nothing has to be considered when building people or should we say no-*thing* should be considered, but the *persons* being built. You build people one person at a time and you build persons by building the peopleness part of them. People being the plural form of person entails the social dimension of personhood. If people did not build people, then people as a plural form would not exist. If persons only built persons then no persons would exist, because it is the law of this world that you need two before you can even get one. But, it is the oneness of the two that makes the one the two make even worth making.

It is the same for social transformation. There would be no point in transforming the social world if there was no social world. There would be no point to transform ourselves individually if there was no collective context in which each individual could reside. A personal transformation that has no social component is incomplete, because as persons we are also people.

Therefore, personal transformation can be looked at as a people transformation and therefore on the same plane as a social transformation. You are merely transforming the social part of a person which is the same on a macro scale as transforming the people part of a society.

It is our social nature that is the more inner part of us. The person part of us is actually more superficial and when we meet person-to-person we are merely connecting at the surface. But when we meet social to social we are no longer separate people, but one person.

The builders are building the buildings that the builder has built inside of them. Built inside of us is the inherent nature to build outside of us. This is a component of our human capacity to imagine. This is our desire to build social relations and engage with the external material world.

Some people withdraw into themselves, but can only do so for so long before they are bankrupt. You can only find so much of you before you see the other in you. The other in you is both you and your inherent relationship with the other.

Within society we see people individually who make up society, but within each of these people we see the social nature of the people that form the nature of the society or the society in them. How long will it take us to realize that society is no different from us in this aspect. Society is something internal to all of us individually and all of us collectively. It is the fruit of our social nature, but also at the root of it too.

We can be no more satisfied with the world than we are interacting with it. It is like complaining about the results of an election when you didn't even vote. It is often the people that are most critical of society that never actually engage with it. Not in the appearance of engagement, but in true engagement.

True engagement is performing the acts that are most inherent within us as social beings. It is building the social beingness of other social beings. It is helping them to transform so that they as part of your society transform the society part within you.

That which is being built is built without hands. It is built by building buildings for the builders that are in the builders and patterned after the building of the great builder them self.

This is the foundation and this is the future. All which rises up upon this will also come from it. There is nothing that can be without this. A pile of tools and supplies could never build itself without builders themselves. A group of builders could never build themselves without tools and supplies. The tools of builders are themselves and their greatest supply is the support of the great supplier of the resultant outcome or transformation they are to be built into.

How is this all done? Is it all metaphysical or what role does the material and or physical world play in the building of the immaterial world of people. Can you have a home without a house? What role does the house play in a home? What role does the body play in the development of the spirit? And, what role does the outward beautification of the social world play in the inward beauty of the social actors within it?

Chapter 46

The Role of the Material World In Social Change

What effect does the material world have on us and our mission? Our mission is to bring about social transformation through personal transformations. Though, as we stated in the last section, true social transformation is first more of an internal thing for a society just as it is first an internal thing for an individual and their own transformations. But, true transformation includes both the internal and external changes.

Do the external changes play an actual role in the internal changes? We have discussed previously in the book that the external world cannot cause change to occur, but can influence it in that it can prepare the environment for change to occur by not preventing change from occurring.

By not demotivating change from occurring, in a way it does motivate it as a concept alone. It can motivate change, but not the changers. But, when the changers see the change they see the need to change and then can choose to change. Thus, the material world can be an instrument of changing the world in that it is used properly as an end in itself and not as a means to change oneself or any other self.

Most of the time we use instruments as means to accomplish a task, but when the task involves humans, instruments must act according to the limitations by which humans act. The human then becomes the means for using the instrument and not the other way around.

For example, one can use beauty as an instrument to promote beauty, but not force beauty, because forcing beauty destroys the essence of beauty as an ideal to be protected. All things that are beautiful, good, or positive and characteristics of a transformed society are beautiful, good, and positive as ends in themselves and therefore need not be used as means for themselves or their own arrivals.

Thus it is of great importance to use the material world as it was meant to be used; which is different than the way it is usually used. We often use the material world for our satisfaction. We feed our bodies, build houses, churches, and cities, but though these things might seem necessary, we will actually find more satisfaction as we become unaware of our feeding and building of the physical structures that support life. As we become so engaged in their relationships with ourselves independently and inter-independently, the food we consume and the buildings we occupy will consume our attention and occupy our minds about as much and is often as we think about air and gravity.

Air is beautiful in that it supports life and therefore so is food. Gravity is necessary in that it holds us in place and therefore so are places. But, the life that is supported and the place that is held are merely open buckets to be filled by the parts of life filled fully whatever their commission is whatever space that is required.

So is the beauty of the Earth and the body. The beauty of the world on the earth and the man in the body. The earth has a purpose just as do our bodies and the rest of the material world. To provide us with a structure in which infinite, eternal, and spiritual beingness could reside. And therefore, the infinite, eternal, and spiritual purpose of these beings is to make where they reside as glorious as they themselves are. Not as a thing to be done, but as a mission that is being fulfilled.

By being transformed internally you are fulfilling your mission. And, by transforming externally you are fulfilling your mission. Thus, the mission is to transform and the mission is ours to perform. Ours, the spirits in the body. The world on the Earth.

C. S. Lewis said, "You do not have a soul. You are a soul. You have a body." As a family, you do not have a home. You are a home. You have a house. As a society, we do not have a world. We are a world. We have an earth.

What does it mean to be a world? To be a home? Or, to be a spirit? We are not the earth. A family is not the house. A person is not their body. The body is the house of the spirit, a house is the body of our home, and the earth is what we live on, but not why we live on, or exist. These things exist independent of their materiality.

Life comes from within. It comes from the spirit within us. To make a house a home is to make a living for yourself and for your family. The earth belongs to all of humanity, not just a few. As it belongs to all, we must all bear a common responsibility for it. All in a home carry certain responsibilities of the house. We as individuals are responsible for our bodies. But, what of this responsibility and why?

Our bodies come from the earth. Our homes are constructed from the earth. Our earth has been organized from eternal elements out of the heavens. It came from above just as much as we do. As we have a responsibility for what we do, we have a responsibility for what we do to it. When material and immaterial are linked, a relationship emerges in which responsibilities come to effect.

The union of body and spirit, house and home, world and earth are related to the responsibility we have for each component separately and together. The death of the body is merely its separation from the spirit. The death of a house is the separation of it from the home. The death of the earth is the separation of it from the world. This is physical death.

The death of a spirit is the separation of it from its maker. The death of a home is a separation of it from its makers. The death of a world is the separation of it from its maker. This is spiritual death.

Both physical and spiritual death are prevalent in our world today, but it is usually only the physical death of people in the earth that goes noticed. Healthcare and environmentalism are two factors of physical death.

Spiritual death goes less noticed because of its spiritual nature of being unobservable in its processes, though its outcomes can be seen. Someone can die physically without dying spiritually and die spiritually without dying physically. People die spiritually when they are openly rebelling against the truth and are therefore not in harmony with it or with those that embody it. The world can die spiritually when people rebel against the truth and against each other. To be at war with their maker is to be at war with society because they being a society are made a society by the social nature of those whom they are trying to destroy.

We will one day all become one, spiritually and physically, individually and collectively, in all things and in all ways, but until then we must will it so by doing so now. As we do it now, we can guarantee that we will do it then. Without present action there will be no future to act in.

It is this that is the fate of the untransformed. It is they who will not share the fate of the transformed, nor be able to act fully and freely because they are not acting fully and freely according to the capacity for acting that they have now and are neglecting. They will have no power over the material world while those of the transformed will both have power over it and in it because they have become one with it. This oneness has been and will be a way of life for them.

Chapter 47

When Will People Change?

As we have stated before, *the most important and urgent change is that people see change to be important and urgent.* Once they see this, change is inevitable. Once change is inevitable it is definite. And when definite change occurs in the way we prescribe, it becomes infinite and everlasting.

People often change when the pain of not changing is greater than the pain of changing. Does change hurt? Yes, usually. Not that it has to, but because we allow it to. As Tim Hansel said, "Pain is inevitable, but misery is optional." Therefore, we can't avoid pain, but we can avoid its misery. Thus, the only thing that can hurt us is us and our own perceptions of pain.

Change most often hurts when the only one reason why the person is changing is due to the rational proposition above. Let's say that someone decided to change before the pain of not changing ever emerged. This is what prominent business consultant Tom Peters meant when he said, "Change before you have to." When this is the reality, pain is absent from the beginning and therefore irrelevant throughout.

Pain comes most when changing when the least amount of change has been made before the change has made you change. One comes by willful choice while the other comes by forceful choice. In forceful choice, one is backed in a corner with only one option out. And, the option out is usually a painful one. But, in their mind not as painful as opting out of the choice to change and staying backed in the corner.

It is those who willfully choose to change before they have to who never find themselves in a corner. Not because they are in a round room, but because they are in the center of whatever room they are in. Just as they are centered in the room they are in, they are centered in themselves their bodies and their spirits.

Being in the center does not hurt. In the center one can fall and hit no wall. In the center one can see an infinite amount of directions to go. In the center, all things are possible even the absence of pain.

This is in essence the argument of whether or not you will choose to be humble or be humbled period. Choosing to be humble always results in true humility, but being humbled results in true humility only if the person chooses what they could have chosen before they were humbled. Someone can be humbled, but not be humble.

They who are humble do not need to be humbled. In fact, if some outward circumstance appeared to have humbled them, they would feel no less humble that they were beforehand because it is impossible for them to be humbled by anything external to them. With this is freedom.

On the flipside some people are in such bondage that no matter how much they are humbled in outward circumstances they will never be humble inwardly, but only by their choice to stay this way.

Staying the way you are when you are not transformed is pride. Staying the way you are when you are transformed is effortless and therefore is nothing to be proud of. Humility is what gets you to that state and what keeps you there. Humility is not knowing that you are there, but also not thinking that you're not. It is no awareness of self and by this non awareness one becomes aware of all things that constitute themselves.

By being aware of the constitution of themselves they know of themselves who they themselves truly are and realize that humbling themselves is not really something that needs to be done because it is what they are and have always been. When they say they are humble they are not bragging, but telling the truth about their nature. Not a nature that was won, but a nature that was given to them as they came from the dust (humus) and are human and humble. They all come from the same root.

Those who humble themselves are really just bearing fruit from the tree that is rooted in the soil that is composed of composted fallen fruits of ages past that lie and die under the tree of life and death.

Humility is the death of the desire not to change and is the changing of one's life into its true life as a humble human from humus.

One can choose to be changed and change to be chosen to change the unchosen and the unchanged by being part of their humbling. But, to be part of this, one can have no part with them in their unchangedness.

To humble someone else, one must be chosen by someone humbler than anyone else. The same that is changed more than anyone else. The same that comes from a realm that is higher than anyone else.

Chapter 48

Why Nothing Else Is As Important or As Urgent

To spread the idea that social transformation can only occur through collective personal transformations is not only an important thing to do in the sense of spreading, but also an important thing to do in the sense of adopting the principles of these types of transformation into one's life. It could well be said the same of its urgency. The application of the knowledge is more urgent than the spreading of the knowledge itself. Now, why is this so and what can looking at alternative solutions tell us about our own?

For an example to illustrate our argument, we will discuss the concept of equality and inequality. If one was to take control of the whole world and equalize it in every way possible and then give control back over to the world, the world would soon become just as unequal as it was before the controlled equalizing took place. Why is this? It is because the actors or human agents that are in control of the resources by which equalization is measured are also in control of the measure of resources they choose to keep or distribute.

Those who were forced to give more than their fair share would in vengeance, through a self-proclaimed act of justice, take back what was their fair share if not more. Those who were undeservedly given more than their fair share would inevitably not stand a fighting chance to be able to keep these, their newly acquired resources. They would have to protect these resources more from the enemies within themselves than from the enemies without.

The courses of action prescribed to each of the parties have been deterministic just as in the way in which the quality was determined by the outside agent of force. Now, after a forced equality such as this, it is not inevitable that the people would react in the ways suggested. It is probable, but it is not impossible for them to act in a different way. Though, acting in a different way would imply some sort of transformation in the way that they saw the problem and in the way that they go about solving the problem.

From the side who supposedly gave up more than their fair share, they could see it as a privilege to give of themselves for the betterment of all. From the other side, the typically more "underprivileged," they would see the gift of getting more than their fair share as a gift and not an entitlement. By them viewing it as a gift, they receive it with gratitude enough to truly own it and cherish it. When the others give it as a gift they truly disown both the responsibility for the resources and the subsequent need for balancing the reciprocity of a forced exchange as such.

Therefore, it is not impossible for even a forced equality to work, but it is not as probable. To make something such as this more probable, the transformations would occur beforehand rather than after the fact.

Trying to encourage them after an attempt of abuse on both sides would be like hitting someone larger than you and expecting them to just turn their cheek. Those who would turn their cheek are those who have already been transformed. It is easy for them to turn their cheek because they have already turned their lives away from the natural reaction to things. And, the reason why we know, if it was to be forced today, that no one, collectively speaking, would turn their cheek, is because if they truly would, we, as a collective society, would already have turned ourselves around in true social transformation.

Thus, we are suggesting that by turning away from the natural attitude and taking upon oneself the transformative attitude, the world of which we are a part would be transformed and equalized in a proper and just manner. And, this equalization would be as sustainable as were the transformations which cause it. And, *that which would bring the world out of balance is that which is keeping it out of balance now.*

Thus we see that any attempt to change the world other than that of through the way we prescribe, social transformation through personal transformations, will always be unsustainable. Only every time. And, the only sustainable way to truly transform the world is for the world to truly transform itself first. Not that transforming itself after the fact is impossible in a theoretical sense, but equally as not probable as it is not impossible.

Basically it's not that it can't happen, but that it won't happen. Yet, on the converse, true social transformation is possible and probable a way so strongly that we can say it is infinitely close to definite if personal transformations happen first, occur simultaneously, and seal the transformation at the end. Thus the transformation is not an event, but a process. And though the completion only happens once, it does not happen all at once. Thus, it can look like an event, but it is really just the visible manifestation of the final part of the mostly-invisible process. It is as was state in the preface of boxing champions. "Champions don't become champions in the ring—they are merely recognized there."

Social transformation is not made by collective personal transformations, but is true when persons collectively recognize its completion. This recognition happens as subtly as falling asleep. No one has ever fallen asleep conscious of their falling asleep.

We must wake up with as much vigor as the schoolboy who wakes up and sees his clock and realizes he is late for class. This book, or the plea of this part of the book, is as the alarm clock that we can either choose to wake up from or choose to snooze. The alarm has been ringing since the day day was made.

We have been sleeping, wasting away the beautiful day of opportunity for too long and instead of taking more sleeping pills, we are inviting the world to wake up to their privileges and to the possibility of doing the impossible and being impractical by saying with us that true social transformation is only one choice away-be it a collective one.

Chapter 49

The One Choice

Albert Einstein once said, "Reality is an illusion, albeit a very persistent one." We say in the same meter, but with different meaning that "transformation is a choice- be it a persistent one." With this, we have now made choice eternal. And, with this choice eternal we have one eternal choice. Or, it could even be rephrased as, "eternal choice number one." Therefore, the choice is the first and the last choice you will ever have to make and it is also all the choices in between. It is, in fact, the only choice you will ever have to make and is therefore the only choice you will ever want to make certain you choose correctly.

What of choice? Choice usually implies that there are at least two options to choose from. But, in this case, there is only one choice to choose. There are no other alternatives, for, by even not choosing, you choose. Therefore, the choice can be summed up as the choice to choose.

This choice to choose is the same as the question posed by Shakespeare. "To be, or not to be?" Being is choosing. Nonbeing is not choosing, but is therefore choosing not choosing, and is therefore choosing. We cannot get away from the beings that we are because even the act of trying to get away is an act of being. What Shakespeare meant by "not to be" was and is the only way to truly get away from being or nonbeing.

One can choose to choose or choose not to choose, but they who never choose either one are they who are not either being or nonbeing. The reason why it is such a question is because it is so perplexing as to why and how this occurs.

The question has in fact already been given to each of us. Choose? That is it. That is the one choice. It makes sense that it is only one word. And, now it makes sense that it is not a statement but a question. The question not posed by us, but by that which made us, that which is making us, and that which will make us into what it already is. It gives us the choice whether to be like it or not be like it. That is the question.

We answer the question throughout our lives in the persistent acting out of the one choice. It is our choice whether to be transformed or to not be transformed. Even the negatively transformed are still transformed. It is the non-transformed that are no longer beings at all. And, it is the reality of our world that this non-beingness in this sense is impossible.

Because, once the question has been posed, which it has to all of us, there is no neutral ground. We chose choice and are therefore asked what we will do with it and therefore the one choice is to continue choosing choice.

The one big choice gets bigger as you choose because so does your capacity to choose. Therefore, the choices themselves get bigger. And, as they get bigger so do they the makers of the choices get bigger.

Thus, the size of the choice we need to make as a society is as big as the society itself. The importance of this choice is as big as is society's capacity to assign importance to anything at all. The urgency to make this choice is as great as is the timetable in which the question was asked. The choice is so urgent that it should have already been made. You are late for school. The choice is yours whether or not to snooze a little more or respond to this alarm.

Those who respond are those who will be respondents to and for the great questionnaire. They will participate in the asking as much as they participate in the answering.

What we choose today determines our choices of tomorrow. And, our choices of tomorrow can be chosen for us by our choices today. When a child makes the choice not to smoke and is offered a cigarette later on in life, the choice is easy because they said no a long time ago. It is the same here.

We invite everyone who is reading this to not only believe what we have said, but to also do what we have said by choosing transformation. To choose transformation is to transform the choice inside of you. It is choosing the only way for sustainable change and is therefore the only way to change sustainably.

Though the choice is infinite, eternal, and spiritual in nature, it is in our present, limited, physical world that we are to make the choice. The choice in the perspective of its nature would be a given and not really a choice at all. It is therefore why we are to choose it under these conditions that makes it a choice at all. The choice was never intended to be easy, because you never learn from that which is easy. More important than being obedient is learning how to choose. When one has learned how to choose fully they have learned what to choose fully and therefore their knowledge and actions can be congruent and obedience no longer becomes an issue but a given.

We have written this book to help promote both of these choices. Choose to learn and choose to obey. And thus, both are essentially a choice and can be boiled down to choosing to choose. And further, choosing to choose choice over non-choice.

This choice to choose is always one choice away from all of us and therefore is simply one choice collectively. To make a choice, choice must exist, must be known, and must be free. Though we know that this choice is the choice to be made, only you can choose to make it.

We say to everyone, "choose transformation" so that the world might be transformed. It is not until we choose that we will become chosen, or transformed by the agent of transformation and the transforming agent, and thus reach a state of sustainable change never to fall again. Therefore, true social transformation can truly only come through *choosing* collective personal transformations, but only always.

www.ingramcontent.com/pod-product-compliance
Lightning Source LLC
LaVergne TN
LVHW020927090426
835512LV00020B/3253